LEEDS UNITED
CHAMPIONS

1991/92

LEEDS UNITED

THE GLORY SEEKERS

Tuesday 13 August 1991

PUBLISHED BY THE YORKSHIRE EVENING POST, OFFICIAL SPONSOR OF LEEDS UNITED 25P

CHAMPIONSHIP GOAL... Leeds United's midfield star David Batty has the First Division title in his sights this season — and he wouldn't mind scoring the odd goal either.

Evening Post

LEEDS UNITED

INSIDE

Howard Wilkinson's Leeds United side made a huge impression on their return to The Big Time last term.

Now it's all systems go to bring some silverware back to the Elland Road trophy cabinet Inside this soccer special, published by the *Yorkshire Evening Post*, the club's official sponsor, our experts focus on:

● New boys Tony Dorigo, a £1.3m signing from Chelsea, Steve Hodge, a £900,000 buy from Nottingham Forest, the Wallace twins Rod and Ray who cost a combined fee of £1.7m from Southampton.

● Goal ace Lee Chapman contemplates a repeat of last season's exploits when he was the leading scorer in Division One.

● Midfield terrier David Batty talks about his club and international ambitions for the new season.

● Plus a look at the prospects for Bradford City, Huddersfield Town, Barnsley, Halifax Town, York City and Scarborough plus Yorkshire's top non-league clubs.

GLORY SEEKERS! The *Yorkshire Evening Post* previews the forthcoming campaign.

LEEDS UNITED
CHAMPIONS

1991 / 92

DAVID SAFFER

TEMPUS

Acknowledgements

I would like to thank the following people and organisations for their help with this publication. Howard Wilkinson for kindly providing the foreword. Mike Fisher at *The Yorkshire Evening Post,* Leeds United Football Club, James Howarth and Fran Gannon. Last but by no means least thanks to Gary Shepherd for producing all the statistics.

To Dad:

For many years we'd followed the fortunes of Leeds United together, but this was a season when we won the ultimate prize. The memories we shared together in the build-up, during and after each game in that 1991/92 campaign will live with me forever.

First published 2003

Tempus Publishing Limited
The Mill, Brimscombe Port,
Stroud, Gloucestershire, GL5 2QG

© David Saffer, 2003

The right of David Saffer to be identified as the Author
of this work has been asserted in accordance with the
Copyrights, Designs and Patents Act 1988.

British Library Cataloguing in Publication Data.
A catalogue record for this book is available from the British Library.

ISBN 0 7524 3112 9

Typesetting and origination by Tempus Publishing Limited
Printed in Great Britain by Midway Colour Print, Wiltshire

1991/92 First Division Fixtures

20 August 1991	Leeds United v. Nottingham Forest
24 August 1991	Leeds United v. Sheffield Wednesday
28 August 1991	Southampton v. Leeds United
31 August 1991	Manchester United v. Leeds United
3 September 1991	Leeds United v. Arsenal
7 September 1991	Leeds United v. Manchester City
14 September 1991	Chelsea v. Leeds United
18 September 1991	Coventry City v. Leeds United
21 September 1991	Leeds United v. Liverpool
28 September 1991	Norwich City v. Leeds United
1 October 1991	Crystal Palace v. Leeds United
5 October 1991	Leeds United v. Sheffield United
19 October 1991	Notts County v. Leeds United
26 October 1991	Leeds United v. Oldham Athletic
2 November 1991	Wimbledon v. Leeds United
16 November 1991	Leeds United v. Queens Park Rangers
24 November 1991	Aston Villa v. Leeds United
30 November 1991	Leeds United v. Everton
7 December 1991	Luton Town v. Leeds United
14 December 1991	Leeds United v. Tottenham Hotspur
22 December 1991	Nottingham Forest v. Leeds United
26 December 1991	Leeds United v. Southampton
29 December 1991	Leeds United v. Manchester United
1 January 1992	West Ham United v. Leeds United
12 January 1992	Sheffield Wednesday v. Leeds United
18 January 1992	Leeds United v. Crystal Palace
1 February 1992	Leeds United v. Notts County
8 February 1992	Oldham Athletic v. Leeds United
23 February 1992	Everton v. Leeds United
29 February 1992	Leeds United v. Luton Town
3 March 1992	Leeds United v. Aston Villa
7 March 1992	Tottenham Hotspur v. Leeds United
11 March 1992	Queens Park Rangers v. Leeds United
14 March 1992	Leeds United v. Wimbledon
22 March 1992	Arsenal v. Leeds United
28 March 1992	Leeds United v. West Ham United
4 April 1992	Manchester City v. Leeds United
11 April 1992	Leeds United v. Chelsea
18 April 1992	Liverpool v. Leeds United
20 April 1992	Leeds United v. Coventry City
26 April 1992	Sheffield United v. Leeds United
2 May 1992	Leeds United v. Norwich City

Foreword by Howard Wilkinson

When I joined Leeds United in October 1988, the long-term strategy was to set the club back on the road to the glory days of the Revie era. We had to get the team, facilities and ground right, but as a one-club city I knew that we had the potential to do it.

Before the start of the 1991/92 First Division campaign I believed we had a chance to win the Championship, because we had performed really well the previous season after winning promotion in 1989/90. We had players who could go out and impress, and possessed in the squad a mixture of youth and experience with David Batty and Gary Speed playing alongside the likes of Gordon Strachan, John Lukic, Lee Chapman and Gary McAllister. Bringing Tony Dorigo, Rod Wallace and Steve Hodge to the club brought more balance to the team and tactically improved our options.

The win at Southampton early on demonstrated to me that we could get results away from home. We embarked on a promising run, losing once in our opening 27 matches, which included great wins over Liverpool, Chelsea and Manchester City. There were also our televised victories at Sheffield Wednesday and Aston Villa, and we did remarkably well to come back in a clash against the defending Champions Arsenal. However, we still found ourselves trailing Manchester United. Our draw against them on Boxing Day was very important, because they could have gone five points clear, which would have been a psychological advantage for them at that stage of the season.

Like all teams we had our injury problems but overcame them, and showed plenty of character especially after Manchester United knocked us out of two cup competitions, and when we were heavily defeated at Queens Park Rangers and Manchester City. Leaving Maine Road, I decided to get the players in the following Monday. We had five games left, and I told them we needed to win four of them, which would put pressure on Manchester United, who I felt sure would drop points having to play four fixtures in six days over Easter.

We went back to the team and shape that had served us so well earlier in the season. Barring tactical differences I'd play that shape come what may. After our draw at Liverpool and win over Coventry City, suddenly the title was in our grasp with Manchester United losing against Nottingham Forest and West Ham.

Before the clash against Sheffield United, I sensed the atmosphere among the players was that if we won, the title was ours. They knew that the result mattered far more than the performance. I tried to keep a lid on it. The game at Bramall Lane defied belief on reflection; it had just about everything. The conditions were difficult, but some of the goals and incidents were unbelievable. We got the right result and within a few hours had been crowned Champions. It was an incredible day.

The players were magnificent throughout the campaign. On occasion they played with injuries and out of position, but that demonstrated the spirit in the side, and in my captain Gordon Strachan we had a great player who was inspirational. His preparation was first rate, and he always put the team first.

My time at Leeds United, and in particular the title successes we achieved were professionally the most satisfying period in my life. I am sure you will enjoy recalling what was a fantastic campaign.

Introduction

Since Leeds United's formation in 1919, on only three occasions have the club won the ultimate domestic honour, the First Division title. Prior to the appointment of Don Revie as manager in 1961, there were four top-10 finishes, the best fifth in 1929/30. Under Revie of course, such statistics were obliterated as his team became the most feared side in England after winning the Second Division title in 1963/64. In a decade when seven teams won the First Division crown, no club could match Leeds United's overall consistency. Never finishing outside the top four, Revie's aces finished runners-up five times and twice claimed the Championship, in 1968/69 and 1973/74.

When Revie departed, Leeds' decline as a major force began. Relegation followed in 1981/82, and the Second Division is where the team languished until the arrival of Howard Wilkinson nine games into the 1988/89 campaign. Under his guidance the renaissance began with the signing of Gordon Strachan, and by the end of the 1989/90 season 'Wilko' had masterminded Leeds' return to top-flight football. During their first season back in the First Division the team surprised many observers by finishing fourth, before stunning everyone by climbing to the summit in 1991/92.

Playing with panache and power, Leeds battled head-to-head with Manchester United. For much of the campaign, the Yorkshire side doggedly hung in behind their Pennine rivals, before finally taking the ascendancy during the key Easter fixtures. As the team from Old Trafford cracked, Wilkinson's team grew in strength, and hours after a 3-2 victory in the penultimate game of the season at Sheffield United, Leeds clinched the title when Liverpool defeated Alex Ferguson's team.

I still recall the highs and lows of a tumultuous campaign, which included many classic encounters as the leadership changed hands seven times between the top two, before Wilkinson's team finally triumphed. Who could forget the historic win against Liverpool or the thrilling encounters with Manchester United and Arsenal, Sheffield Wednesday's annihilation, a quite extraordinary game at Sheffield United and the 'Mexican wave' celebrations against Norwich City when the 104-year-old trophy returned to Elland Road.

It is a remarkable story, and in this book the players' exploits are recollected. No Leeds United supporter who witnessed the matches will ever forget Strachan's drive, Chapman's hat-tricks, Batty's never-say-die attitude, McAllister's elegance, Lukic's agility, Speed's versatility, Wallace's pace, Fairclough and Whyte's composure, Sterland and Dorigo's swashbuckling

displays, Hodge's cameo roles and finally Cantona's 'goal in a million'.

Every match is covered in detail, along with comprehensive statistics and over 100 illustrations of a magnificent campaign when Leeds United once again ruled the English game.

Enjoy the memories.

David Saffer

Pre-Season

Since taking over the reins at Leeds United in October 1988, in his 34 months as manager, Howard Wilkinson had invested £10.4 million on 26 players, whilst 30 players had generated £3 million. During the 1991/92 close season £4.2 million of talent had bolstered the Leeds squad led by his most inspirational signing, skipper Gordon Strachan.

With 'new boys' including Rod Wallace (£1.6m), Tony Dorigo (£1.3m) and Steve Hodge (£900,000) joining the likes of John Lukic, Lee Chapman, Mel Sterland, Chris Fairclough, Gary McAllister, David Batty and Gary Speed, Leeds now had one of strongest squads in the League that appeared capable of challenging for honours.

Confidence was high within the club and spectators were looking forward to an exciting campaign. Season ticket sales of £3.4m was up on the previous season and 1990/91's total of 21,200 season ticket holders would also be exceeded.

Fortunes for the club had certainly improved with the announcement of a £10 million sponsorship deal with Admiral, due to start at the beginning of 1992/93 when the club's current deal with *Yorkshire Evening Post* expired. With gates expected to break through the 20 million barrier for the first time since 1980/81, there was no better time to be following the 'beautiful game'.

For the first time in 16 years, there would also be three Yorkshire sides in the top division with Leeds, Sheffield United and Sheffield Wednesday battling it out for superiority in their own mini-league. Pre-season odds had Leeds down at 10-1 fourth favourites behind Liverpool 13-8, Arsenal 15-8 and Manchester United 8-1; however, the Leeds boss stayed well clear of predictions when looking ahead to the new campaign in the *Yorkshire Evening Post* pre-season special *The Glory Seekers:*

'You have got to attack things in stages and for me that means when the season starts your first target is the number of points you think will be enough to keep you up. You cannot have a vague distant horizon in your mind that you hope will come near to you at some stage. You have to have something that people can see – your first goal, first point, first victory. These are all things that players understand. When you get sufficient points to stay up then you have a go for it on the basis that you think what you have done in the summer has improved your squad. I think that overall we have a better squad than we did last season so we have to look for an improvement on what we did last season.'

Following a pre-season schedule that included a World Soccer '91 Challenge match against the Brazilian side Botafoga at the Tokyo Dome, Wilkinson was looking forward to the opening league game of the season at Crystal Palace. However, with everything set for the big kick-off, the club was left reeling three days before the season's opener at Selhurst Park when the match was suddenly postponed due to 'ongoing redevelopment work'. After failing to get permission for the game to be played behind closed doors, or gain the points due to Palace not fulfilling their obligations to the League, United's manager labelled the decision 'astonishing and disgusting'. Incensed, the club hastily arranged a friendly with Aldershot to give Wilkinson's squad match practice and whilst the rest of the First Division began their campaign, Wilkinson and his assistant Mick Hennigan took the opportunity to watch their opening two opponents Nottingham Forest and Sheffield Wednesday in action.

Leeds United v. Nottingham Forest

20 August 1991
Elland Road, Leeds

Football League, First Division
Attendance: 29,457

On the eve of the club's opening fixture against Nottingham Forest, Howard Wilkinson told *Yorkshire Evening Post* reporters, 'No matter how hard you work in pre-season games, they do not have the same 'bite' as a league game. It's always difficult in your first game and it is something of a relief to get the first one out of the way.'

Announcing a fully fit squad, Wilkinson chose to leave new boy Steve Hodge on the bench, though Tony Dorigo and Rod Wallace would both make their league debuts.

LEEDS UNITED opened their league account with a hard-fought win over Forest thanks to a goal by Gary McAllister, but they were also indebted to a number of superb saves from John Lukic in goal.

Leeds and Forest ran out to a backdrop of fireworks and it soon became apparent that both sets of players were fired up for this match. The home side settled quickly and deservedly took the lead on 13 minutes following a long throw-in by David Batty. Lee Chapman caused the damage, winning an aerial battle with Steve Chettle to set up McAllister, who fired home from the edge of the penalty area. It was a well-worked move and clinically finished, no doubt making Brian Clough rue the day he failed to persuade the talented midfielder to join him before his move to Elland Road in 1990.

With neither side dominating midfield, supporters were unable to relax throughout the match. Forest had their chances either side of the break, but Lukic denied them on each occasion, frustrating Stuart Pearce, Gary Charles and Scot Gemmill. Leeds had their opportunities too and looked unfortunate to be denied a penalty when Chapman was challenged clumsily by Carl Tiler. At the finish Leeds players were clearly delighted to have got off to a winning start.

United's skipper Gordon Strachan was as inspirational as ever, but Man of the Match was

Tony Dorigo. Assured in defence, he supported intelligently down the left flank, giving balance to the side. With early signs of a promising partnership developing between Chapman and Rod Wallace, Leeds showed why they were being tipped as 'dark horses' for Arsenal's league crown.

Referee: N. Midgley (Bolton)

Howard Wilkinson, *Yorkshire Evening Post*: 'Forest played well, especially in the first 20 minutes of the second half, but I thought there were times in the match when you could tell that we had not had a game. This was a good one to get out of the way. Had we not been at our fighting best we might well have lost.'

Leeds United 1
McAllister

Nottingham Forest 0

LEEDS UNITED v. NOTTINGHAM FOREST

HEADS I WIN! Skipper Gordon Strachan gets the better of Scot Gemmill.

IT'S THERE! Gary McAllister crashes home the only goal of the match.

Leeds United: Lukic, McClelland, Dorigo, Batty, Fairclough, Whyte, Strachan, Wallace, Chapman, McAllister, Speed

Nottingham Forest: Crossley, Charles, Pearce, Chettle, Tiler, Keane, Crosby, Gemmill, Clough, Sheringham, Jemson

LEEDS UNITED v. SHEFFIELD WEDNESDAY

24 August 1991
Elland Road, Leeds

Football League, First Division
Attendance: 30,260

The first top-flight derby in 22 years between these two Yorkshire rivals was eagerly awaited. To add spice to the encounter, both Howard Wilkinson and former Leeds favourite John Sheridan, who made over 250 appearances during the 1980s, would face their former clubs for the first time.

Despite the hype the Leeds boss was confident he could detach himself from an emotional occasion and was expected to name an unchanged team. United skipper Gordon Strachan was well aware of the danger posed by Sheridan but was confident that David Batty would be able to prevent that from happening.

IN A BELOW-PAR PERFORMANCE Leeds were indebted to super-sub Steve Hodge's late strike for a share of the spoils.

The match got off to a cracking start with Lee Chapman just failing to convert a cross from Rod Wallace, and Gary McAllister shooting narrowly wide from a couple of strikes on goal. It was the visitors though who carved out the best chances, but on each occasion Paul Williams snatched at his opportunities when well placed.

With Leeds struggling to stamp their authority on the game the tension affected the players, who found it difficult to settle down. David Batty had to leave the field briefly for treatment to a leg injury, but was soon back in the thick of the action.

Leeds nearly broke the deadlock on the half-hour when Chris Woods saved brilliantly from Gary Speed's shot following Chapman's lay-off. As the players departed for half-time, Wednesday were clearly the happier and it was no surprise when David Hirst gave his team the lead on 48 minutes. Put in the clear by Paul Warhurst, the powerfully built Hirst beat Chris Fairclough with ease before lashing the ball past John Lukic for a fine goal. The 18-year-old, who Howard Wilkinson snapped up for £250,000 from Barnsley, was giving Leeds' central defenders a torrid time and could have added to his tally, but slack finishing let him down. Indeed, his goal was the hardest of his opportunities.

With Wednesday looking comfortable, Wilkinson made a double substitution on 68 minutes. Mel Sterland replaced John McClelland and Steve Hodge came on for Gary Speed. Suddenly Leeds had a zip about them with Sterland charging down the right flank and Hodge breaking from midfield. With time running out it appeared that the players may experience one of those days, but three minutes from time Leeds finally got the break their endeavour deserved. Gordon Strachan might not have been at his sharpest, but when a clearance fell to him his header caused panic in the Wednesday defence. For the first time, Nigel Pearson was caught in two minds and misjudged his clearance. Hodge raced in to stab the ball past Woods from 12 yards.

Leeds were off the hook but there could be no doubting their work ethic. Wilkinson's team demonstrated why they would be a tough team to beat; they kept battling and sent supporter's home satisfied.

Referee: C. Trussell (Liverpool)

Leeds United 1
Hodge

Sheffield Wednesday 1
Hirst

SUPER SUB! Steve Hodge grabs a late equaliser in the Yorkshire derby.

Lee Chapman loses out in this aerial battle as Leeds attack.

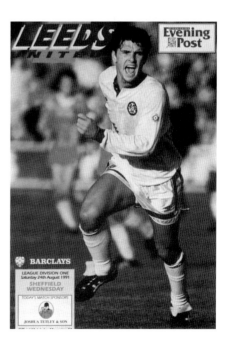

Leeds United: Lukic, McClelland (Sterland 68), Dorigo, Batty, Fairclough, Whyte, Strachan, Wallace, Chapman, McAllister, Speed (Hodge 68)

Sheffield Wednesday: Woods, Nilsson, King, Palmer, Warhurst, Pearson, Wilson, Sheridan, Hirst (Francis 90), Williams (Anderson 89), Worthington

LEEDS UNITED v. SHEFFIELD WEDNESDAY

GOAL!

Howard Wilkinson, *Yorkshire Evening Post*: 'We made far too many passes and finished up with a lot of hard lines, but in the end deserved a point.'

Steve Hodge, *Yorkshire Post*: 'I scored in my debuts for Villa and Tottenham. This one fell nicely to give me 100 per cent on debut goals away from Forest. It's unusual but it's a nice habit.'

SOUTHAMPTON v. LEEDS UNITED

28 August 1991
The Dell, Southampton

Football League, First Division
Attendance: 15,847

One player who was relishing this clash was Rod Wallace, who put in ten transfer requests before being allowed to leave The Dell. Speaking to the *Yorkshire Evening Post* he said, 'I know that I will be a marked man but I am looking forward to the game. Southampton have long been known for having a leaky defence so maybe I can find a way through.'

Tactically, Howard Wilkinson was looking for his midfield players to get into the opposition penalty box on a more regular basis. He also warned his players that apart from Matthew Le Tissier, their promising young striker Alan Shearer 'could play a bit' also.

TWO GOALS APIECE from Gary Speed and Gordon Strachan in a bruising encounter on the South Coast, which saw Neil Ruddock dismissed, enabled Leeds to record their biggest win at The Dell in nearly 70 years.

From the kick off, Leeds were first to settle and soon had a stranglehold on the game, but after 17 minutes they had to reshape their defence following an injury to Chris Fairclough after a clash with Russell Osman. Initially switching places with David Batty to run off the knock, it proved impossible. Mel Sterland came on at right-back as John McClelland switched to centre half alongside Chris Whyte.

The changes were seamless as Leeds continued to dominate possession. Rod Wallace went close against his former team, as ex-United star Micky Adams did for the Saints, but it was Leeds who opened the scoring when Speed thumped home a drive on 23 minutes from 14 yards, after Ruddock had failed to control Sterland's cross.

Much the happier side at the interval, the visitors began the second period in sensational fashion, with both Lee Chapman and Gary McAllister striking the woodwork. The game exploded into action on 56 minutes when Ruddock's challenge on Wallace resulted in a penalty for Leeds and a sending off for the rugged centre-back. With new directives for referees, Ruddock's dismissal was mandatory. Wallace was clean through on goal, so the red card was the only decision. Strachan made no mistake from the spot kick.

With the Saints reduced to ten men, Leeds were now cruising. Twenty minutes from time, another clumsy challenge in the penalty area, this time from Osman on Chapman, brought a second penalty award of the evening, but no red card. Again Strachan was clinical.

With the game safe, it was a major disappointment when McAllister, who had been superb all evening, had to be carried off with a nasty looking injury after he misjudged a tackle just four minutes from time. There was further joy though for United followers when Speed fired home a 30-yard thunderbolt in the dying moments of the game.

Referee: G. Ashby (Worcester)

Howard Wilkinson, *Yorkshire Evening Post*: 'We will have to wait and see how they (McAllister and Fairclough) come along, but at the moment it does not seem that either will be fit to play [on Saturday], but you never know.'

Southampton 0

Leeds United 4
Speed (2)
Strachan (2 Penalties)

SOUTHAMPTON *v.* LEEDS UNITED

CLOSE CALL! Saints keeper Tim Flowers clears the ball before Lee Chapman pounces.

Southampton: Flowers, Dodd, Osman, Horne, Hall, Ruddock, Le Tissier (Lee 79), Cockerill, Shearer, Rideout (Moody 59), Adams

Leeds United: Lukic, McClelland, Dorigo, Batty, Fairclough (Sterland 17), Whyte, Strachan, Wallace, Chapman, McAllister (Hodge 86), Speed

Manchester United v. Leeds United

31 August 1991
Old Trafford, Manchester

Football League, First Division
Attendance: 43,778

Although only the fourth game of the season, this was one fixture that every Leeds supporter looked forward to and would be a major test.

Alex Ferguson made no secret that the League Championship was his number one priority. The last time his club had won the title was in 1967, and although his side had won the FA Cup and European Cup Winners Cup during the previous two seasons, this was the honour he craved. Adding Peter Schmeichel, Paul Parker and Andrei Kanchelskis to his star-studded outfit, the Old Trafford manager knew he had a team capable of ending the title bogey.

Leeds' rise to prominence in recent seasons had made teams take notice; indeed Bryan Robson described this 'Roses' clash as the 'acid test'. With both sides protecting unbeaten league runs, this was going to be some battle, and depending on how Manchester City and Coventry fared, a victory for either side could see them top the League.

With, as expected, Chris Fairclough failing to recover, John McClelland partnered Chris Whyte in central defence, enabling Mel Sterland to make his first start of the season. Shortly before kick off Gary McAllister was pronounced fit.

LEE CHAPMAN'S FIRST-HALF GOAL earned Leeds a share of the spoils in an exciting 'Roses' battle played on a day better suited to sunbathing than watching a football match.

In sweltering conditions, which touched 80 degrees, the match began at a furious pace. Leeds more than held their own, and stunned their rivals with a goal from Chapman after seven minutes. Tony Dorigo began the move with a high ball down the left flank to Gary Speed, who swung a superb cross away from the goalkeeper. Peter Schmeichel misjudged the flight of the ball enabling Chapman, completely unmarked, to head home at the far post.

With Leeds dominant in midfield, Alex Ferguson had plenty to ponder especially when Paul Ince limped off after 21 minutes. Ryan Giggs came on and immediately gave Sterland problems with a fine run and shot, which only just missed the target. Moments later the 17-year-old's pace almost caught the out Leeds defence again, but John Lukic saved comfortably. Though the home team enjoyed plenty of possession, David Batty and Rod Wallace flashed a couple of long-range efforts just over the bar as Leeds showed they could be dangerous on the counter-attack.

Manchester began the second period in blistering fashion and should have equalised within minutes of the restart when Giggs shot wide after Mark Hughes had set him up. His miss was the start of sustained pressure, and the Leeds goal appeared to have something of a charmed life. Hughes missed a sitter, Clayton Blackmore struck a post and Lukic denied Giggs. It was 'backs-to-the-wall' for the Leeds defence, but they coped admiringly as Bryan Robson drove his team forward.

Four minutes from time the home side's relentless pressure paid off when Robson pounced after Lukic had saved brilliantly from Brian McClair. A draw was just about right. It had been a heroic performance by Leeds, who came so close to a famous victory.

Referee: K. Redfern (Whitley Bay)

Howard Wilkinson, *Yorkshire Post*: 'It was a long hard trip on Wednesday (from Southampton), and we did not get back until 2.30 a.m. on Thursday. Today heat was a telling factor and we started to play tired and I suppose it was a typical Manchester home surge. They dug deep.'

Manchester United 1
Robson

Leeds United 1
Chapman

MAN ON! Gary Speed battles for possession with Bryan Robson.

Manchester United: Schmeichel, Parker, Irwin, Bruce (Phelan 76), Webb, Pallister, Robson, Ince (Giggs 23), McClair, Hughes, Blackmore
Leeds United: Lukic, Sterland, Dorigo, Batty, McClelland, Whyte, Strachan, Wallace, Chapman, McAllister (Hodge 80), Speed

FIRST BLOOD! Lee Chapman nods Leeds ahead at Old Trafford.

	P	W	D	L	F	A	Pts
Manchester United	5	3	2	0	5	1	11
Liverpool	5	3	1	1	7	4	10
Manchester City	5	3	1	1	7	5	10
Nottingham Forest	5	3	0	2	10	6	9
Tottenham	4	3	0	1	8	6	9
Leeds United	4	2	2	0	7	2	8

CLOSE CALL! Gary Speed is thwarted by Peter Schmeichel.

LEEDS UNITED v. ARSENAL

3 September 1991
Elland Road, Leeds

Football League, First Division
Attendance: 29,396

Hot on the heels of playing one of the title favourites, Leeds entertained the defending champions Arsenal. Twice winners in the previous three seasons, this would be a searching test for Wilkinson's players, but having played the Gunners six times in 1990/91, including four epic FA Cup ties, Leeds knew they could compete.

Surprisingly Arsenal had begun the campaign poorly, but Leeds skipper Gordon Strachan warned against complacency in the *Yorkshire Evening Post*. 'If Arsenal are considered to have problems, then I think nearly every team in the land would love to have their problems. Up to a couple of weeks or so ago the Gunners were widely accepted to be the best team in the land, and a team who have just won the title does not suddenly become a bad team overnight.'

IN A THRILLING ENCOUNTER, Leeds showed all their battling qualities after going two goals behind to claim a share of the points with a Gordon Strachan penalty and a late goal from Lee Chapman.

Leeds began the game brightly and should have taken an early lead through Chapman on 11 minutes, but after beating Andy Linighan with ease he shot wide when well placed. The miss soon proved costly when George Graham's side deservedly took the lead on 20 minutes, Paul Merson setting up Alan Smith whose first time shot from the edge of the penalty area gave the Leeds 'keeper no chance. Although Strachan probed and encouraged, Arsenal looked comfortable during the remainder of the half.

Three minutes after the break the Gunners took a tight grip on the game. Again it was Merson who caused the damage with a brilliant run. Finding Nigel Winterburn, the left-back's shot was cleverly redirected by Smith again to put the visitors two goals ahead. The goal rocked Leeds, and but for inspired goalkeeping by John Lukic, who denied Kevin Campbell, Winterburn, Michael Thomas and David Rocastle, Arsenal would have added to their lead.

Suitably encouraged, and driven on by Strachan, Leeds slowly came back into the game and got a break with 25 minutes to go, when Lee Dixon, under pressure from Rod Wallace, handled on his goal line. Gary McAllister forced the ball home, but the referee had already given a penalty. Strachan who had scored two penalties at Southampton converted with ease. Although open to the counter-attack Leeds had nothing to lose and put Arsenal under immense pressure. With 12 minutes remaining Steve Hodge replaced Mel Sterland in a desperate bid to grab a point.

Three minutes from time Leeds equalised. David Batty began the move, McAllister neatly headed the ball over Arsenal's static defence for Chapman to nip in and score from close range. Arsenal were stunned, and astonishingly Chapman nearly won the match with an overhead kick that just shaved the angle of bar and post.

Man of the Match for Leeds had been McAllister, who was involved in everything, including a stint as an emergency right-back when Sterland needed stitches for a leg injury. The comeback was no more than the home side's battling display deserved in a pulsating match.

Referee: B. Nixon (West Kirby)

Leeds United 2
Strachan (Penalty)
Chapman

Arsenal 2
Smith (2)

LEEDS UNITED v. ARSENAL

GENTLY DOES IT! Lee Chapman completes a brilliant comeback against the Gunners.

Howard Wilkinson, *Yorkshire Evening Post*: 'If you look at the football side of the game we deserved to get something out of it. Some people might say we were lucky to get away with it, but we played some tremendous stuff. It showed that you can never write my team off. Looking at the game and the way we were playing we were forced to get a goal. It had to come, it was inevitable.'

George Graham, *Yorkshire Evening Post*: 'The penalty was the deciding factor because they poured forward after that and took their chances. He (Lukic) made five outstanding saves, several of them in one-to-one situations, and that for a home 'keeper is unusual.'

Leeds United: Lukic, Sterland (Hodge 78), Dorigo (Wetherall 90), Batty, McClelland, Whyte, Strachan, Wallace, Chapman, McAllister, Speed
Arsenal: Seaman, Dixon, Winterburn, Thomas (Rocastle 78), Linighan, Adams, O'Leary, Davis, Smith, Merson, Campbell

LEEDS UNITED v. MANCHESTER CITY

7 September 1991
Elland Road, Leeds

Football League, First Division
Attendance: 29,986

With four out of their next six games away from home, Leeds were determined to depart with a home victory under their belts. Playing against the team lying second in the table, Leeds boss Howard Wilkinson was well aware that his team would be in for a tough match, however after recent performances against the two title favourites, confidence was high in the squad. With Chris Fairclough out for a few weeks, Wilkinson named an unchanged side from the one that performed so well against Arsenal.

A THUNDEROUS STRIKE by Tony Dorigo, his first for the club, and a rare David Batty goal, only his second goal in 161 appearances for Leeds, were the highlights of this impressive home win. Bizarrely, Batty's last strike was also against Manchester City on Boxing Day 1987; his latest goal put Leeds well on the way to a comfortable victory.

The early stages of the game saw Rod Wallace and City's flying winger David White look dangerous. Sadly for Leeds, Wallace pulled up sharply with a groin injury after 12 minutes to be replaced by Steve Hodge. Within six minutes however, Leeds had scored the opening goal, and what a scorcher.

Gordon Strachan's corner appeared to have been safely cleared by City's defence when it was headed out towards Dorigo on the left edge of the penalty area. Watching the ball carefully, Leeds, left back gave City 'keeper Tony Coton no chance with a sensational volley into the top corner of the net. Clearly encouraged, Lee Chapman almost extended Leeds, advantage when Gary McAllister played him through, but his shot was far too weak to trouble Coton.

The home side was looking irresistible and they doubled their lead on 35 minutes. The only surprise was the goalscorer. Again Strachan was the architect with a lovely through ball, which Batty latched onto. Just when everyone thought the twenty-two-year-old would pull the ball back across the goal for players in support, the Leeds anchorman slid the ball home from a tight angle.

Two goals behind City tried to get back into the game, and their perseverance almost paid off when they were awarded a penalty on 67 minutes after Chris Whyte was adjudged to have fouled Niall Quinn just inside the penalty area. Unfortunately for the Blues, although Peter Reid scored from a rebound after his spot kick had hit the post, nobody else had touched the ball so the goal was disallowed.

It was a schoolboy error by City's player-manager but it summed up his day, which got worse when his missed tackle led to Leeds' third goal after 80 minutes. Batty's tenacity won their final midfield duel, before his pin-point pass set up Hodge, only for Steve Redmond to scythe him down for the second spot kick of the afternoon, which Strachan converted for his fourth penalty in as many games.

This had been an impressive performance by Leeds and especially Batty, his display overshadowing even Dorigo's scintillating strike. The win moved Leeds up to fourth place in the table, the only blot being that Wallace would be out of action for up to six weeks.

Referee: I. Cruikshanks (Hartlepool)

Leeds United 3
Dorigo
Batty
Strachan (Penalty)

Manchester City 0

SCORCHER! Tony Dorigo is delighted with his strike against Manchester City.

Leeds United: Lukic, Sterland, Dorigo, Batty, McClelland, Whyte, Strachan, Wallace (Hodge 12), Chapman, McAllister, Speed

Manchester City: Coton, Hill, Pointon, Reid, Curle, Redmond, White, Brightwell, Quinn, Megson, Brennan (Heath 46)

PERFECTION! David Batty scores Leeds, second with a great finish.

David Batty, *Yorkshire Evening Post*: 'It's never bothered me not scoring. I was actually going down so I just hit the ball and it went in. I thought I would have been leaping over the wall to celebrate, but the reaction of the crowd was such that I actually found it hard to concentrate for a while afterwards. I felt a bit sorry for Tony (Dorigo). He scored a great goal but I pinched the limelight.'

	P	W	D	L	F	A	Pts
Manchester United	7	5	2	0	10	2	17
Liverpool	6	4	1	1	9	5	13
Manchester City	7	4	1	2	9	5	13
Leeds United	6	3	3	0	12	4	12

LEEDS UNITED v. MANCHESTER CITY

Niall Quinn is marshalled by his opposite number Lee Chapman as City try to get back into the match.

14 September 1991   Football League, First Division
Stamford Bridge, London   Attendance: 23,439

With five Leeds players on international duty, there was precious little time for Howard Wilkinson to prepare for the trip to Stamford Bridge; however, he was not complaining, despite the logistical problems. Speaking to the *Yorkshire Evening Post* he said, 'It's good for the individuals, the club and our supporters, but it makes the manager's job difficult. My big test during the next day or two is lifting those who are down, getting others to get their feet back on the ground and generally making sure they all concentrate their energies and attention on the task ahead at Stamford Bridge.'

Whilst Leeds players would be playing against former team-mate and crowd favourite Vinnie Jones, Tony Dorigo was relishing his return. The Leeds boss's biggest dilemma all week had been who he should partner with Lee Chapman in Rod Wallace's absence. Carl Shutt was available after a seven-week lay-off, but with only 45 minutes reserve-team football behind him, he was not match fit. In the end Wilkinson decided to gamble on his semi-fit striker.

CARL SHUTT MADE A STUNNING RETURN TO THE FIRST TEAM, scoring the only goal in a tough battle at Stamford Bridge. The result sent Leeds soaring to second place in the table.

Chelsea, adapting quickly to the humid conditions, had the game's opening chance, but Kevin Wilson fired wide from Dennis Wise's cross. Leeds slowly came into the game, but the best they could muster were two long-range efforts from Gary Speed and Gordon Strachan.

With David Batty and Vinnie Jones closing down attacking opportunities, chances were at a premium, although Chris Whyte appeared fortunate to get away with a challenge in the penalty area on Chelsea legend Kerry Dixon. Just on half-time though both sides had an opportunity to break the deadlock, Speed having a header smartly saved by Kevin Hitchcock, and Dixon just missing Wilson's cross when clear of his marker.

The hot weather was one of the main reasons for the pedestrian pace; however, just past the hour Leeds took the lead with the games best move of the match. Strachan and Gary McAllister were involved in the move before Shutt headed Speed's perfect left-wing cross home. The goal galvanised Chelsea and their supporters, who urged their team forward. As the game intensified, both Batty and Wise were fortunate to only receive a warning from referee Roger Milford after one 'tasty' clash. This was not a game for the faint-hearted.

As expected Tony Dorigo received jeers from the home crowd at every opportunity, but the former Chelsea hero turned saviour for Leeds when his pace enabled him to deny Graeme Le Saux a tap in after Dixon's shot went across the face of the goal. Three minutes from time, Wise thought he had grabbed an equaliser from close range after Le Saux's astute pass, but fortunately for Leeds he was ruled offside.

The final whistle brought relief for Leeds' travelling army of supporters in what had been a tight contest. It may not have been pretty to watch, but all the top teams were now aware that Leeds United were powerful, determined, organised and mighty difficult to beat.

Referee: R. Milford (Bristol)

Chelsea 0   Leeds United 1
                                         Shutt

CHELSEA v. LEEDS UNITED

BATTLE AT THE BRIDGE! Gary McAllister takes on former Leeds hero Vinnie Jones.

Leeds United: Lukic, Sterland, Dorigo, Batty, McClelland, Whyte, Strachan (Hodge 75), Shutt, Chapman, McAllister, Speed

Chelsea: Hitchcock, Clarke, Boyd (Dickens 67), Jones, Elliot, Monkou, Le Saux, Townsend, Dixon, Wilson (Allon), Wise

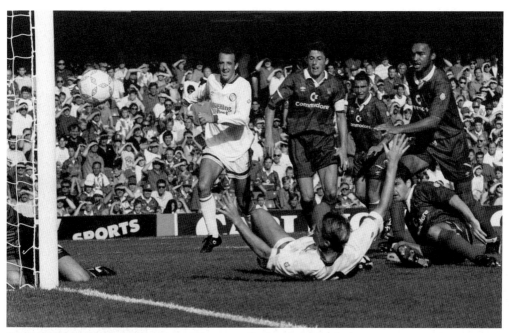

GOAL REF! The referee rules that this Lee Chapman strike hasn't crossed the line.

WELCOME BACK! Carl Shutt nods home the winner.

MOVE IT! The referee orders Shutt to return for the kick-off or he's in trouble.

Carl Shutt, *Yorkshire Evening Post*: 'At first I thought the referee had disallowed the goal, but he was referring to me running towards the fans. I told him I'd been out of action for eight weeks and asked him what he would have done if he had scored a goal after being out for so long. He then told me to carry on.'

COVENTRY CITY v. LEEDS UNITED

18 September 1991
Highfield Road, Coventry

Football League, First Division
Attendance: 15,488

Leeds prepared for their midweek clash against a rejuvenated Coventry side, sitting fourth in the table after wins over Arsenal and Notts County. There were injury doubts over both Gordon Strachan and Mel Sterland but eventually both players were passed fit to play.

Coventry may have been, somewhat unusually for them, riding high early in season but manager Terry Butcher was well aware of the challenge ahead. In an interview with the *Yorkshire Evening Post*, the former England stalwart said, 'When you go through the Leeds team player by player, it is a frightening thought. Leeds will give us a big test. It will be physical and their players will have the right attitude and battle hard. They play very disciplined football.' Signalling United's skipper for special praise Butcher said, 'He has a great deal of experience and is a very influential captain. Other players gain strength from him. Strachan is a real extension of Howard Wilkinson on the field and is totally committed to the way Leeds play.'

JOHN LUKIC'S OUTSTANDING START TO THE SEASON continued with a breathtaking save from Robert Rosario and a fifth clean sheet as Leeds extended their unbeaten record to eight games with a resolute away display. The point gained emphasised Leeds defensive qualities, and their unbeaten start is now their best since they won the First Division crown in 1973/74.

At the start of this match Coventry appeared more intent on avoiding defeat than going for a win but on their rare excursions into attack they quickly found the Leeds 'keeper in imperious form. Commanding in his penalty area from dangerous crosses throughout the half, Lukic excelled himself following a corner on the stroke of half-time. How he managed to save Rosario's effort on goal must still be puzzling the centre-forward, but somehow United's 'keeper dived to his left to pull off a sensational save. The look of disbelief on Rosario's face said more than the save itself.

In the second half, defences again dominated. Lukic was called upon a number of times, but especially 13 minutes from the end when Kevin Gallacher broke through. Fortunately for Leeds, Lukic was quick to spot the danger and made a fine save.

Unfortunately for the Scottish striker, he injured his knee in the fifty-fifty challenge and was stretchered off before being taken to hospital for an X-ray.

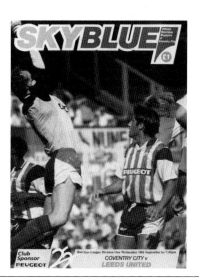

Leeds will feel this game was one they should have won though, and they would have, had they converted one of a number of gilt-edged chances. Lee Chapman, normally so clinical in front of goal, had three opportunities, especially seven minutes from time when he headed wide from close range after Mel Sterland's superb centre had evaded Coventry defender's. Nevertheless, it had been a solid performance by Leeds, with John McClelland, in particular, faultless as he continued his impressive form in the absence of Chris Fairclough. His manager must be glad he has such an experienced and competent back-up defender.

Referee: D. Axcell (Southend-on-Sea)

Coventry City 0   Leeds United 0

COVENTRY CITY v. LEEDS UNITED

OH NO! Lee Chapman misses a late chance to snatch a win.

Howard Wilkinson, *Yorkshire Evening Post*: 'John (Lukic) had another faultless evening. Apart from his notable save (from Rosario) and another deflected shot, which could have been a problem, everything he had to do was routine goalkeeping but very important routine goalkeeping. Crosses into the box he came for and took cleanly, and fifty-fifty balls with people coming into the box he took competently.'

	P	W	D	L	F	A	Pts
Manchester United	8	6	2	0	11	2	20
Leeds United	8	4	4	0	13	4	16
Chelsea	9	4	3	2	15	11	15
Coventry City	9	4	2	3	13	7	14

Coventry City: Ogrizovic, Borrows, Billing, Robson, Pearce, Atherton, McGrath, Gynn, Rosario, Gallacher (Ndlovu 78), Furlong
Leeds United: Lukic, Sterland, Dorigo, Batty, McClelland, Whyte, Strachan, Shutt (Hodge 74), Chapman, McAllister, Speed

Leeds United v. Liverpool

21 September 1991
Elland Road, Leeds

Football League, First Division
Attendance: 32,917

For this eagerly awaited clash, a capacity crowd of 32,728 was guaranteed. The most recent encounter between the two clubs in April saw the Reds win an incredible match 5-4 after leading 4-0 at half-time. Not surprisingly the match was the hottest ticket in town!

The game would be Gordon Strachan's 100th league appearance for Leeds since joining in March 1989. His impact at the club had been akin to Bobby Collins in 1962, which heralded Don Revie's great side. In the *Yorkshire Evening Post* on the eve of the clash Strachan said, 'I could hardly have wished for a better fixture than one against Liverpool to mark this personal milestone. Time flies when you are enjoying yourself. It must be the quickest 100 games I will have played anywhere. A new club has been formed during that time. There is a new stature about Leeds these days. This club of ours is going up and up.'

His manager said of his skipper: 'There is no drop in his output, no drop in his quality. So long as he keeps thinking as positively as I do about the situation, he will continue to turn in the performances he is capable of producing, the sort we require.'

Arguably the most intriguing clash of the day would be to see how the Leeds defence, so tight in recent games, would fare against Ian Rush and their £2.9 million striker Dean Saunders, especially after Leeds withdrew a £3 million bid during the close season following his former club's delaying tactics.

There was one change to the Leeds team line-up. With Carl Shutt rested, Gary Speed was asked to play in attack alongside Lee Chapman, enabling Steve Hodge to fill the left midfield slot for his first start of the season.

A TERRIFIC FIRST-HALF VOLLEY by Steve Hodge brought Leeds their first victory over their great rivals for 18 years, generating a standing ovation and wild celebrations from ecstatic supporters at the final whistle.

This was a significant victory for Howard Wilkinson's team, their first over one of the 'big guns' (Manchester United, Arsenal and Liverpool) since their return to top-flight football. Leeds' win kept them second in the table, with another clean sheet to boot, their fourth in succession and sixth in nine games.

Quickly into their stride, Leeds should have taken an early lead on 11 minutes when Gordon Strachan's cross caught Bruce Grobbelaar in no man's land. Lee Chapman's lob beat the 'keeper only to be cleared off the line. It didn't take the home side long though to make the breakthrough when Hodge marked his first start with a clinical strike on 25 minutes. The build-up to the goal had started with a Strachan corner that Grobbelaar came for, but failed to clear. When the ball eventually fell to Tony Dorigo on the edge of the penalty area, Hodge expertly hooked his cross into the top corner of the net. It was a fantastic strike.

Within minutes Gary Speed almost created a second goal for Hodge, but after laying on a wonderful pass from the right flank, Hodge's shot was well blocked by Steve Nicol. Little had been seen in the opening half from Liverpool's strikers, but credit must go to Leeds centre-backs John McClelland and Chris Whyte for keeping the Welsh duo quiet. The look on both managers' faces as they walked off for the interval told the story of the first period.

Graeme Souness's team talk had an immediate impact as Liverpool upped their game on the resumption, but his side was unable to seriously threaten John Lukic's goal. The biggest

Leeds United 1	Liverpool 0
Hodge	

LEEDS UNITED v. LIVERPOOL

MY BALL! Gary McAllister and Rob Jones jostle for possession as Rod Wallace looks on.

disappointment for the Reds was the ineffectiveness of wingers Steve McManaman and Mark Walters who rarely featured. Leeds looked comfortable, and deserved a second goal to make the game safe. Their best chance fell to Strachan on 80 minutes when he was sent clear by Gary McAllister's astute pass, but Grobbelaar, one-handed, magnificently saved his shot.

The miss nearly proved costly four minutes from time when David Batty lost possession to Dean Saunders, but the Liverpool striker's snap shot failed to trouble Lukic. The frustration clearly got to the Liverpool camp and led to referee George Courtney lecturing Souness. However, an equaliser would have been rough justice on Leeds, now second favourites at 4:1 behind Manchester United at 13:8.

Referee: G. Courtney (Spennymoor)

	P	W	D	L	F	A	Pts
Manchester United	9	7	2	0	16	2	23
Leeds United	9	5	4	0	14	4	19
Tottenham	7	5	1	1	15	9	16
Sheffield Wed	9	5	1	3	15	10	16

Leeds United: Lukic, Sterland, Dorigo, Batty, McClelland, Whyte, Strachan, Hodge, Chapman, McAllister, Speed (Shutt 73)
Liverpool: Grobbelaar, Ablett, Burrows, Nicol, Marsh, Jones, Tanner, (Harkness 35), Saunders, Rush, Walters (Rosenthal 65), McManaman

GLORY MOMENT! Steve Hodge seals Leeds' first win over Liverpool for eighteen years.

Howard Wilkinson, *Yorkshire Evening Post*: 'You only had to see how our spectators reacted to our victory over Liverpool to realise just how important it was to so many people, but that game is now just a statistic. The next game is the most important one.'

Gordon Strachan, *Yorkshire Evening Post*: 'Liverpool have a fantastic tradition and wonderful players and it gives you a kick when you beat them. While we may think our victory over them was extra special it is really just another big step along the road in our bid to get back to the top.'

Steve Hodge, *Yorkshire Post*: 'It was nice to get the goal, it's a nice scalp for us, but they'll be there at the end of the season'.

Graeme Souness, *Yorkshire Post*: 'It disappointed me that we did not capitalise on the late chance Saunders had, but all credit to Leeds. They deserved to win, they were better than us in most departments.'

Bruce Grobbelar claims the ball before it reaches Gary Speed and Lee Chapman.

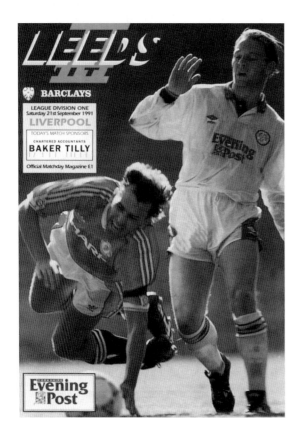

NORWICH CITY v. LEEDS UNITED

28 September 1991
Carrow Road, Norwich

Football League, First Division
Attendance: 15,828

With Gordon Strachan ruled out of the clash at Carrow Road following an injury in a draw at Scunthorpe United in the Rumbelows Cup (second round first leg), the question occupying supporters minds was who would captain Leeds in his absence. The general consensus was that the honour would go to either John McClelland or Gary McAllister. In the end it was something of a surprise when David Batty was handed the captains armband. One further surprise by United's manager was naming Imre Varadi as Strachan's replacement, most pundits expecting Carl Shutt to be recalled. Shutt had to be satisfied with a place on the bench.

CLINICALLY TAKEN GOALS by Tony Dorigo and Gary Speed should have won this highly entertaining encounter, but slack defending cost Leeds two points as Dale Gordon's brace grabbed the Canaries a share of the spoils.

With United's stand-in skipper David Batty prominent during the early stages, Leeds troubled the Norwich defence with a number of attacks in the opening 20 minutes. Dorigo in particular was causing danger every time he joined the attack and from one such sortie, Gary McAllister headed just over the bar. Imre Varadi also went close, before Steve Hodge had an effort well saved.

The home side almost made the visitors pay shortly before half-time when Ruel Fox was clear on goal. Fortunately for Leeds, instead of passing, John McClelland managed to get back to block Fox's goal-bound shot. It had been a lucky escape for Leeds, who enjoyed territorial advantage in the second half until the home side took a shock lead against the run of play on 58 minutes. Gordon grabbed the goal, after neat interplay with Fox, giving John Lukic no chance with a low shot. This was the first goal the Leeds 'keeper had conceded in over nine hour's play since the league clash against Arsenal.

The goal snapped Leeds into action and they were soon back in the game when Dorigo equalised from a well-worked free kick. McAllister, Speed and Mel Sterland acted as decoys, before the cultured left-back crashed home a tremendous left-foot strike past the motionless Bryan Gunn. Norwich came back at Leeds and forced Lukic to make further saves from Gordon and Rob Newman. However, on 72 minutes Leeds appeared to have rapped up the points when Chris Whyte returned Gunn's clearance over Norwich's static defence for Speed to race clear and coolly give his team a deserved 2-1 lead. Unfortunately for the visitors, within two minutes of a topsy-turvy encounter there was one last twist when Gordon grabbed his second goal after winger Robert Ullathorpe set up a simple chance.

Referee: P. Jones (Quorn)

	P	W	D	L	F	A	Pts
Manchester United	10	8	2	0	18	3	26
Leeds United	10	5	5	0	16	6	20
Arsenal	10	5	2	3	23	15	17
Sheffield Wed	10	5	2	3	16	11	17

Norwich 2
Gordon (2)

Leeds United 2
Dorigo
Speed

Norwich City v. Leeds United

GOTCHA! Norwich' keeper Bryan Gunn clasps the ball as Steve Hodge looks to strike.

Howard Wilkinson, *Yorkshire Post*: 'We let the game slip and paid the penalty. It gradually went away from us. We can't do anything about what Manchester United or Arsenal or any of the others are doing, but what we have achieved so far gives us a good basis on which to build.'

Norwich City: Gunn, Phillips, Bowen, Butterworth, Blades, Crook, Gordon, Fleck, Newman, Fox, Ullathorne

Leeds United: Lukic, Sterland, Dorigo, Batty, McClelland, Whyte, Varadi (Shutt 73), Hodge (Whitlow 85), Chapman, McAllister, Speed

TAKE THAT! Lee Chapman thunders in a shot as Leeds chase a winner.

CRYSTAL PALACE v. LEEDS UNITED

1 October 1991	Football League, First Division
Selhurst Park, London	Attendance: 18,298

After the postponement of this fixture on the opening day of the season, Leeds' rearranged clash against Crystal Palace offered an opportunity to close the gap on Manchester United, involved in European Cup-Winners Cup action. With Ian Wright having departed to Arsenal, £1.8 million striker Marco Gabbiadini would be keen to impress on his league debut.

LEEDS CRASHED to their first defeat of the season when Mark Bright scored the only goal of a hard-fought encounter deep into injury time. The loss will have delighted league leaders Manchester United, still six points clear, and now having the benefit of a game in hand.

With only one victory at Selhurst Park in 60 years, it was never going to be easy for Leeds, and without Gordon Strachan, they struggled to make inroads. Andy Gray was the pick of the midfield players with David Batty and his England colleague Geoff Thomas cancelling each other out. Linking well with his defence and making intelligent runs, Gray was a constant threat to Leeds. Though Leeds fought manfully, the home team had the better openings in the first half, forcing their lofty opponents to hang on grimly at times, and will have been disappointed not to have taken an interval lead.

Leeds closed down Palace better in the second period, but as an attacking force they rarely threatened. For the Eagles, Bright looked sharp but Marco Gabbiadini struggled to make an impact and found difficulty staying on his feet when challenged; a point not unnoticed by Leeds defenders. It was from one such incident that the only goal of the game came, when John McClelland was adjudged to have fouled him. The tackle appeared innocuous enough, but Gray made Leeds pay dearly with a terrific ball into the six-yard area that Bright converted for the winner.

For a game that was hard fought, but never dirty, Leeds' manager will have been disappointed that four of his players were booked. Injury worries must have also been prominent in his thoughts, with Gary McAllister the latest player to join the club's injury list with an ankle injury eight minutes from time.

Referee: J. Martin (Alton)

Howard Wilkinson, *Yorkshire Evening Post*: 'We took the best Palace could throw at us in the first 45 minutes, and then never looked like conceding a goal. The goal was only their second strike in the second half.'

Steve Coppell, *Yorkshire Evening Post*: 'Leeds are one of the strongest sides in the division. They lost their playmaker Gordon Strachan and that was our good fortune. He adds that little bit of invention that you just cannot cater for sometimes.'

Crystal Palace 1	**Leeds United 0**
Bright	

IT'S MINE! Steve Hodge and Gareth Southgate fight for possession.

Crystal Palace: Martyn, Southgate, Sinnott, Gray, Young, Thorn, Osborn, Thomas, Bright, Gabbiadini, Salako (Collymore 9)
Leeds United: Lukic, Sterland, Dorigo, Batty, McClelland, Whyte, Varadi (Shutt 73), Hodge, Chapman, McAllister (Whitlow 85), Speed

LEEDS UNITED v. SHEFFIELD UNITED

5 October 1991
Elland Road, Leeds

Football League, First Division
Attendance: 28,362

Following their midweek defeat to Crystal Palace it was crucial that Leeds bounced back straight away. Although it was still early in the season, European qualification was a big target for the club. With Manchester United facing Liverpool and Arsenal in consecutive games, and Leeds playing some of the League's 'lesser' teams in Sheffield United and Notts County, it was imperative to capitalise on any dropped points from the league leaders.

On the eve of the 'derby' clash against his old adversary Dave Bassett, Howard Wilkinson had a number of players nursing injuries. Resources were stretched to the limit at Elland Road. As things transpired only Gary McAllister was passed fit to play.

IN A QUITE EXTRAORDINARY GAME Leeds nearly threw away a four-goal lead, following two goals apiece from Mel Sterland and Steve Hodge, before scrambling to an improbable 4-3 win.

It was a bizarre match, as disbelieving Leeds fans watched in horror the comeback of the season from a never-say-die Sheffield United, who belied their place in the Division with an impressive second-half performance. With Manchester United held by Liverpool at Old Trafford, the win reduced the deficit at the top of the table, but it had been mighty close.

Howard Wilkinson's patched-up side began the match in storming fashion when Hodge opened the scoring on five minutes, after Paul Beesley failed to clear Sterland's throw-in. The ball fell invitingly to the Leeds midfielder, still deputising for Gordon Strachan, before threading his shot through a crowded penalty area to give his side the perfect start.

With Gary McAllister dominating midfield Leeds had plenty of possession, and when Blades 'keeper Phil Kite misjudged his positioning on the edge of his penalty area, referee Mr Barrett awarded a free kick for hand-ball. Sterland gleefully fired home his opening goal of the season. It wasn't long before Leeds' right-back had the opportunity to double his tally, when the referee penalised Ian Bryson's clumsy challenge on Tony Dorigo after 37 minutes. McAllister somewhat amusingly argued for the right to take the spot-kick, but Sterland exerted his authority and coolly picked his spot to put his team 3-0 up at the interval.

Both sides made a change at the start of the second half, Mike Whitlow replacing McAllister, whilst the visitors brought winger Dane Whitehouse on for defender Charlie Hartfield.

Two minutes into the half Hodge knocked in his second goal following a free kick from Whitlow. With a 4-0 lead fans speculated on how many Leeds would score. However, Sheffield began to win more possession, with Whitehouse in particular making an impression and it was no surprise when the winger set up Jamie Hoyland to head home a simple chance. The goal unsettled Leeds. Dave Bassett refreshed his attack on the hour with the introduction of Carl Bradshaw. An ankle injury to Sterland on 71 minutes brought Chris Fairclough's return to first-team action, but he was left stranded within five minutes when Carl Shutt's wayward pass enabled Tony Agana to score comfortably.

Suddenly, Leeds looked hesitant. Sensing a chance, and encouraged by their army of supporter's, the Blades tore into Leeds, and were quickly rewarded when John Lukic's poor clearance on 83 minutes was punished by Bradshaw to set up a 'Grandstand' finish. Despite one or two nervy moments Leeds managed to hold on, but there was a huge sigh of relief at the final whistle from shell-shocked home supporters.

Referee: K. Barrett (Coventry)

Leeds United 4
Hodge (2)
Sterland (2)

Sheffield United 3
Hoyland, Agana
Bradshaw

LEEDS UNITED v. SHEFFIELD UNITED

Three Sheffield defenders thwart Lee Chapman as a
dangerous cross sails over the bar.

Leeds United: Lukic, Sterland (Fairclough 71), Dorigo, Batty, McClelland, Whyte, Hodge, Shutt,
  Chapman, McAllister (Whitlow 46), Speed
Sheffield United: Kite, Hartfield (Whitehouse 46), Cowan, Gannon, Gayle, Beesley, Bryson,
  Hoyland, Agana, Booker, Lake (Bradshaw 56)

CATCH ME IF YOU CAN! Gary Speed evades the attentions of Paul Beesley.

PHEW! Steve Hodge looks relieved to have scored, but he's just put Leeds 4-0 ahead!

Howard Wilkinson, *Yorkshire Evening Post*: 'I am just glad to have the match over and the three points in the bag. That provided proof that goals don't make great games. It was no classic. When we had to take off first Gary McAllister and then Mel Sterland with injuries, we lost our shape and rhythm. To say that I was relieved at the final whistle is an understatement.'

	P	W	D	L	F	A	Pts
Manchester United	11	8	3	0	18	3	27
Leeds United	12	6	5	1	20	10	23
Arsenal	11	6	2	3	26	17	20
Sheffield Wed	12	6	2	4	21	14	20

Notts County v. Leeds United

19 October 1991
Meadow Lane, Nottingham

Football League, First Division
Attendance: 12,964

Following an aggregate win in the Rumbelows Cup over Scunthorpe United (3-0) and a week's break for international fixtures, Leeds began preparations for their trip to Notts County where Howard Wilkinson would be returning to the club he had guided to promotion in 1981.

County boss Neil Warnock paid a glowing tribute to his predecessor in the *Yorkshire Evening Post*. 'He deserves all the praise he gets after guiding three clubs into the First Division, and I see Leeds pushing Arsenal and Manchester United all the way in the Championship race. We are going to have to be on top form to get anything out of the game, and I can say for certain that if we squander chances and give away silly goals, as we have in the last few games, Leeds will punish us.'

As expected Gordon Strachan and Mel Sterland returned, but due to John McClelland's late withdrawal, Chris Fairclough lined up. However, the Leeds boss decided not to risk Gary McAllister, Steve Hodge retaining his place in the side.

SUBSTITUTE GARY McALLISTER'S STUNNING 35-YARD STRIKE and a rare goal from Chris Whyte were the highlights of an accomplished display by Leeds United. With Manchester United again being held, two points now settle the top two teams as the title race gathers pace.

Notts County started brightly and employing the 'long-ball' tactic utilised the speed of Kevin Bartlett and Tommy Johnson. Bartlett should have given his side an early lead when Gary Lund capitalised on a poor clearance by John Lukic, but fortunately for Leeds he was wide of the mark. Encouraged, the home side pushed forward and deservedly opened the scoring on 13 minutes when Johnson flicked on Dean Yates' free kick for Lund to score on his top-flight debut with a neat goal from close range. The goal galvanised Leeds, who levelled within six minutes following a well-worked set piece. Gordon Strachan was the instigator with a pinpoint corner. Whyte and Carl Shutt combined to set up Lee Chapman for his first goal in eight games.

Undeterred, County put Leeds under intense pressure and were unlucky not to regain the lead. Craig Short wasted their first opportunity; heading a corner over from eight yards, then when a long ball caught out United's central defenders, Lukic raced out to thwart Bartlett. Shortly after, Tony Dorigo's speed saved Leeds, before Mel Sterland looked relieved when he diverted Mark Draper's shot agonisingly wide of the post.

Warnock had warned his players that missed chances would be punished, and his worst fears were realised when Leeds took the lead against the run of play on 29 minutes. Steve Hodge caused the damage when he met Sterland's free kick perfectly to power home his fifth goal in as many games – making him the club's leading scorer. Ahead for the first time, the visitors almost increased their lead when Whyte just missed the target following David Batty and Shutt's endeavours; however, Leeds breathed a

Notts County 2
Lund
Johnson

Leeds United 4
Chapman, Hodge
Whyte, McAllister

SWEET MOMENT! Chris Whyte grabs Leeds' third and his only goal of the campaign.

sigh of relief moments before the interval when Yates headed just over from a corner to end an exciting half.

The second period began with Gary McAllister on as a replacement for Chapman, due to a back strain. If County thought Leeds' attack would be blunted they were sadly mistaken. With Gary Speed deputising at centre-forward, United were soon on the attack and after forcing a corner, Whyte stretched their lead with a stooping header from Strachan's fine cross. Two goals ahead, Leeds had their best spell of the match and McAllister emphasised the difference in class with a sensational strike after 56 minutes. Leeds were now safe and though Johnson reduced the arrears with a low drive just past the hour, they never looked in danger of surrendering their advantage, despite a nasty looking ankle injury to McAllister, which resulted in him being stretchered off after 70 minutes. It had been a spirited performance by County, who made Leeds fight hard for the win, but in the end class told.

Referee: B. Hill (Kettering)

Notts County: Cherry, Palmer, Paris, Short (Dryden 46), Yates, Draper, Thomas, Turner, Lund (Regis 70), Bartlett, Johnson
Leeds United: Lukic, Sterland, Dorigo, Batty, Fairclough, Whyte, Strachan, Shutt, Chapman (McAllister 46, replaced by Kamara 70), Hodge, Speed

LEEDS UNITED v. OLDHAM ATHLETIC

26 October 1991
Elland Road, Leeds

Football League, First Division
Attendance: 28,199

Having originally pulled out of the Zenith Data Systems Cup, a change of heart saw Leeds play Nottingham Forest, but their interest was soon over following a 3-1 defeat. However, the match did see Rod Wallace return earlier than planned and score in his 40-minute work-out.

The clash with Oldham could potentially see Leeds top the table for the first time in 17 years with Manchester United facing a tricky match at Sheffield Wednesday. The situation was not lost on Howard Wilkinson in his pre-match interview with the *Yorkshire Evening Post*. 'The most important thing as far as I am concerned is that we play well and win. If we do that then we can reflect on anything that may follow.'

The return of Wallace and Gary McAllister saw Wilkinson name what many considered to be his first-choice XI. With Steve Hodge failing a late fitness test, Chris Kamara joined Carl Shutt on the bench.

AN OWN GOAL by Brian Kilcline took Leeds to the top of the table for the first time since 1974 in a dour game at Elland Road. With Manchester United losing 3-2 at Hillsborough, Howard Wilkinson's team could look down from the summit of the First Division.

During the early exchanges Leeds battled away in midfield, but created very little, the only chance spurned by Gary Speed, his header well wide from eight yards after fine interplay by Gordon Strachan and Gary McAllister. Oldham had a defensive grip on the game, but could attack at pace, especially through Rick Holden. Twice he broke through but fired wide when well placed. With a reputation for set pieces, the Lancashire team were always a danger, which centre-back Kilcline demonstrated when he thumped a header against the bar from Nick Henry's corner.

Kilcline's header apart, the opening period had created few scoring opportunities, indeed neither goalkeeper had a shot of note to save. Denying Leeds space in midfield, and leaving no gaps for Lee Chapman and Rod Wallace to exploit, Oldham's tactics had worked to

perfection. The visitors almost grabbed the lead at the start of the second half, but a brilliant one-handed stop by John Lukic after 48 minutes denied Mike Milligan's snap shot from the edge of United's penalty area.

Leeds were in need of inspiration, and McAllister finally created the breakthrough on 55 minutes. David Batty began the move with a crunching tackle on Earl Barrett near the halfway line. Playing the ball to McAllister, the Scot had Oldham's defence retreating with a penetrative run before floating a teasing cross towards Chapman three yards out. The Leeds centre-forward couldn't miss, but before he could touch the ball home, Kilcline in a desperate attempt to clear the ball, smashed it into the roof of the net to break the deadlock.

Suitably encouraged, Chapman and Speed went close with headers as the home team finally took a grip on the game. In the last quarter, Speed was agonisingly wide before departing ten minutes from time following a hefty challenge, replaced by Kamara.

Leeds United 1
Kilcline (OG)

Oldham Athletic 0

THANKS MATE! Brian Kilcline's own goal sends Leeds to the top of the table.

Leeds' supporters greeted the final whistle with relief, and the mood soon changed to elation on hearing the result from Hillsborough.

Referee: D. Allison (Lancaster)

Howard Wilkinson, *Yorkshire Evening Post*: 'Oldham's tactics were difficult to break down, but once they went a goal down they found it difficult to re-adjust. We have worked hard to get where we are; now we have to prove to everyone we are not one-hit wonders. I have never been at the top of the First Division, so it is something entirely new to me, but sometimes when a team gets to the top people ask if they can stay the course. It is a very pleasant surprise and a tremendous feeling to be in front, but being in front does not mean you are going to stay in front. It is vital that we keep getting good results until Christmas, because we have played enough games now to be able to say to ourselves that, given a fair run of the ball, we can have a say in this title race. Now other things are going to be tested, such as depth of the squad, and the ability to be consistent and get results despite difficulties.'

	P	W	D	L	F	A	Pts
Leeds United	14	8	5	1	25	12	29
Manchester United	13	8	4	1	21	7	28
Manchester City	14	8	1	5	19	17	25
Arsenal	13	7	3	3	29	18	24

Leeds United: Lukic, Sterland, Dorigo, Batty, Fairclough, Whyte, Strachan (Shutt 87), Wallace, Chapman, McAllister, Speed (Kamara 81)
Oldham Athletic: Hallworth, Kilcline (Palmer 83), Barlow, Henry, Barrett, Jobson, McDonald, Marshall, Sharp, Milligan, Holden

WIMBLEDON v. LEEDS UNITED

2 November 1991
Selhust Park, London

Football League, First Division
Attendance: 7,025

As Leeds prepared for their clash with the Dons they were boosted by a 1-0 victory over Tranmere Rovers in the Rumbelows Cup. One absentee was David Batty, due to a foot infection that would sideline him along with Steve Hodge, who was still struggling with a groin strain. On a positive note, Gary Speed had recovered from an ankle injury and Rod Wallace had come through his return to the side in the victory over Rovers.

Off the field speculation was mounting that Leeds were about to sign Mo Johnson from Rangers in a £2 million deal, but neither camp would officially comment. One player definitely on the move was midfielder Chris Kamara. With his prospects of first-team football limited, he accepted an offer to join Luton Town for £150,000.

LEEDS UNITED GAINED A POINT from an uneventful affair that failed to lift a sparse crowd at Selhurst Park, but lost their top spot after Manchester United defeated Sheffield United.

United followers could have predicted a frustrating night as their team had failed to record a victory on their ten previous visits to the ground. Nevertheless the 7,000 die-hard supporters who turned up for this clash deserved far more entertainment than what was on offer.

Chances throughout the match were at a premium, with only four shots of note in total. For Leeds the best opportunity fell to Gary McAllister, after fine play by Chris Whyte and Rod Wallace, but the Scot fired over when well placed. As for Wimbledon, Leeds will have prepared for their 'route one' tactics, and defensively handled the aerial bombardment well, but they were still somewhat fortunate to survive on a couple of occasions.

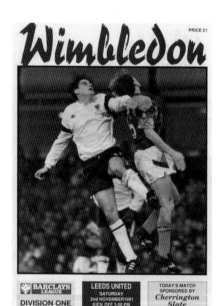

Steve Anthrobus was guilty of a glaring miss after John Fashanu had struck the crossbar just before the break, but by far the clearest opportunity fell to Terry Gibson when clean through in the last minute. His effort though was wide of the target. It was a let off for Leeds, but it would have been an injustice if they had lost. This was not a match for the connoisseur, but a hard-earned point had been gained.

Referee: A. Gunn (South Chaley)

Wimbledon 0

Leeds United 0

NO WAY THROUGH! Rod Wallace tries to get the better of his opposite number.

Howard Wilkinson *Yorkshire Evening Post*: 'I can't speak for Wimbledon, but ours was a tired display from a tired team. The players are disappointed with the result and with their performance, but some of my players have played 20 games already this season, and we are already into November. At the hotel on the morning of the game they looked as though they were preparing for a marathon dance contest, not a game of football.'

	P	W	D	L	F	A	Pts
Manchester United	14	9	4	1	23	7	31
Leeds United	15	8	6	1	25	12	30
Manchester City	15	9	1	5	22	12	28
Sheffield Wed	15	7	4	4	26	18	25

Wimbledon: Segers, Elkins, Phelan, Barton, Scales, Fitzgerald, Ardley, Earle, Fashanu, Gibson, Anthrobus

Leeds United: Lukic, Sterland, Dorigo, Shutt, Fairclough, Whyte, Strachan, Wallace (Newsome 83), Chapman, McAllister, Speed

LEEDS UNITED v. QUEENS PARK RANGERS

16 November 1991
Elland Road, Leeds

Football League, First Division
Attendance: 27,087

Transfer talk was rampant at Elland Road. With Mo Johnson's arrival still being strongly denied, rumours circulated that Hull City's Andy Peyton was now a £1 million target. However, after investing during the summer, fringe players like Bobby Davison and Andy Williams would first have to be off-loaded from the 'full-time' squad of 33 professionals.

Meanwhile, ITV announced that they would be televising Leeds' clash at Aston Villa live on *The Match* and potentially fixtures against Tottenham, Manchester United, West Ham and Sheffield Wednesday. Of more immediate concern to Howard Wilkinson though was the fitness of the first-team squad, which for once reported a clean bill of health following international duty. The Leeds boss had set an objective for the team to reach 40 points by the halfway point of the season; it was not over-ambitious with 10 points required from six games.

PERSEVERANCE WAS THE KEY as two goals within four minutes midway through the second half finally put paid to stubborn resistance from the West London club. Goal scorers for Leeds were Mel Sterland and Rod Wallace, the 2-0 victory returning Leeds to top spot following a draw in the Manchester derby.

Leeds began the match in a sprightly fashion and would have opened the scoring in the first minute had Lee Chapman better controlled a half-chance that came his way. Keeping up the pressure, only a fingertip save by Jan Stejskal kept out a blistering 25-yard shot from David Batty. With Rangers not penetrating in attack, Leeds dominated possession. Chapman nodded over when well placed and Gary Speed headed inches wide as chances were squandered.

Early in the second half Stejskal pulled off a sensational save to deny Speed, but was unable to stop Sterland's deflected free-kick on 58 minutes after Darren Peacock had been penalised for climbing all over Chapman. Sterland's shot may have had a little help on the way, but he was not complaining with his fourth of the season, as it took him two goals clear

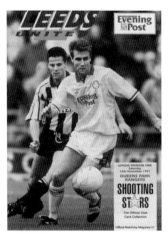

of his personal dual with fellow full-back Tony Dorigo. Within four minutes the advantage was doubled when Sterland turned on Gordon Strachan's corner for Wallace to force over the line from close range for his first league goal of the campaign. After coming back from injury this was a welcome boost to his confidence.

On 68 minutes Imre Varadi replaced Speed, who had an ankle injury, but Leeds controlled the final quarter of the game, the only threat coming when Gary Penrice's close-range effort was brilliantly clawed away by John Lukic. This may not have been the most fluent of performances, but winning whilst finding your form is a nice position to be in.

Referee: K. Breen (Liverpool)

Leeds United 2
Sterland
Wallace

Queens Park Rangers 0

YES! Mel Sterland has finally broken the deadlock against stubborn resistance.

AT LAST! David Batty congratulates Rod Wallace after his goal finished off QPR.

Howard Wilkinson, *Yorkshire Evening Post*: 'Rangers were unbeaten in their last six away games, do not concede many goals and are very difficult to break down. It was important that we did not become impatient. From that point of view I was delighted with the performance. There have not been many occasions in the past couple of months when we have not had to chop and change the side, and given those circumstances the players deserve an enormous amount of credit. Only John Lukic, Tony Dorigo and Chris Whyte have played in all our matches, so the boys in the squad really have done a fine job in getting us up where we are.

Late on I heard the boos when we played for time, but the stakes are high at the moment. My players are honest players striving to give an honest display. If they think passing back is the best thing to do for the result, then they will do it.'

Leeds United: Lukic, Sterland, Dorigo, Batty, Fairclough, Whyte, Strachan, Wallace, Chapman, McAllister, Speed (Varadi 68)
Queens Park Rangers: Stejskal, Bardsley, Wilson, Tillson, (Wilkins 64), Peacock, Maddix, Holloway, Barker, Thompson (Ferdinand 64), Penrice, Sinton

ASTON VILLA v. LEEDS UNITED

24 November 1991
Villa Park, Birmingham

Football League, First Division
Attendance: 23,666

Leeds' televised clash on ITV's *The Match* was eagerly awaited as it featured two of the form sides in the League. Villa with five successive wins behind them had rapidly climbed the table from sixteenth to fourth, but their manager Ron Atkinson was not underestimating the challenge ahead when speaking to the *Yorkshire Evening Post*. He said, 'Leeds will be as big a test as we will have all season. While Manchester United may have an eye on Liverpool and Arsenal, they will probably see Leeds as their main danger in the battle for the title.'

As for Howard Wilkinson, he told reporters. 'Everyone wants to be top of the table. We are there and want to stay there, Villa will be striving to get there themselves. Being at the top of the league is the best position in football. Everyone wants to knock you down, of course, but Liverpool have had that for 20 years or more.'

With Gary Speed's ankle failing to respond to treatment Wilkinson surprised pundits by switching Chris Fairclough to midfield in preference to Steve Hodge. John McClelland partnered Chris Whyte in defence.

THE MOST COMPLETE PERFORMANCE of Howard Wilkinson's tenure saw Leeds brush aside in-form Villa with four goals in a sensational display. The victory took Leeds back to the top as their title odds shortened again to 3:1 second favourites behind Manchester United 5:2, with Arsenal 11:4 and Liverpool 10:1.

Lee Chapman led the way with two goals, but every player was a hero as Wilkinson's charges demonstrated to watching millions their ability to mount a sustained Championship challenge with fast-flowing football, tactical acumen and a non-stop work ethic.

Early on Villa attacked at every opportunity, but United's defence held firm. On the attacking front, Gary McAllister in particular was causing problems with his clinical passing. As both teams probed, Leeds took a firm grip on the match with goals either side of half-time. Rod Wallace grabbed the first after 40 minutes, pouncing on a loose ball after Les Sealey had failed to hold Chapman's header from a Mel Sterland cross. Deservedly ahead Leeds doubled their advantage when Sterland turned goal scorer, nodding home Chris Whyte's flick-on from a Gordon Strachan corner a minute after the interval.

Villa endeavoured to get back into the game, but Leeds were unstoppable. From another intricate corner Strachan and McAllister linked brilliantly to set up a simple tap-in for Chapman on 56 minutes. Gordon Cowans came on after 67 minutes and within 60 seconds home supporters had a brief moment to savour when Dwight Yorke finished off good work by Tony Daley, who robbed David Batty in midfield.

A minute from time Leeds re-established their authority with a sensational goal. Strachan and Sterland created the opening with a fast counter-attack down the right flank, Chapman heading home the full back's pin-point cross with aplomb to seal a superb win.

Referee: A. Buksh (London)

Aston Villa 1
Yorke

Leeds United 4
Wallace, Sterland
Chapman (2)

AGONY AND ECSTASY! Villa 'keeper Les Sealey looks aghast as Rod Wallace scores.

Howard Wilkinson, *Yorkshire Evening Post*: 'Initially we had to work hard because Villa were in full song and obviously very confident. We gradually made room, time and space to start to play in difficult conditions because it was not a good pitch.'

Gordon Strachan, *Yorkshire Evening Post*: 'It was our best performance of the season and to be out there as captain was a great feeling. I am very proud, not only of the fact that we've gone back to the top, but the way we did it. The image of this club means a lot to me and to turn on a performance like that in front of millions of viewers was tremendous.'

	P	W	D	L	F	A	Pts
Leeds United	17	10	6	1	31	13	36
Manchester United	16	10	5	1	25	8	35
Manchester City	17	9	3	5	24	19	30
Aston Villa	17	8	3	6	23	19	27

Aston Villa: Sealey, Kubicki, Staunton, Teale, McGrath, Richardson, Daley, Regis, Atkinson, Blake (Cowans 67), Yorke

Leeds United: Lukic, Sterland, Dorigo, Shutt, Fairclough, Whyte, Strachan, Wallace, Chapman, McAllister, McClelland

Aston Villa v. Leeds United

THREE'S A CROWD! Strachan, McAllister and goalscorer Chapman celebrate Leeds' third.

IN CONTROL! Tony Dorigo keeps abreast of two Villa defenders on a Leeds sortie.

HOWZAT! Lee Chapman seals a fantastic performance with Leeds' fourth goal.

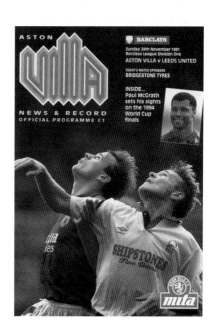

Leeds United v. Everton

30 November 1991
Elland Road, Leeds

Football League, First Division
Attendance: 30,043

The team's victory against Aston Villa dominated headlines for a few days and it came as no surprise when ITV announced Leeds' clash with Manchester United would be covered live on *The Match*. Financially the club would benefit to the tune of £145,000 compared to the £45,000 they received for appearing in a televised match as the away team.

Howard Wilkinson quickly brought the players back down to earth. Speaking in the *Yorkshire Evening Post* he said. 'I can understand people getting carried away with our performance, but I think Leeds fans are sensible enough to know that each game stands on its own. I think they also appreciate they are supporting an honest team that goes out and does its best each week. Last Sunday the team did its best and produced a game which was a real gem, and they will go out against Everton hoping to do the same. Whether or not it happens you never know, but having got the result they did it at Villa Park, they know they are capable of it.'

TEN-MAN LEEDS stayed top when they snatched a late win thanks to a brilliant volley from Rod Wallace seven minutes from time after Chris Fairclough had been controversially dismissed after 69 minutes.

This hard-fought victory against a resolute Everton side was one of their fiercest examinations this season. Their performance could not have contrasted more to the swashbuckling display at Villa Park, but the result was just as significant. In the space of six days the players had demonstrated their desire to entertain or battle as circumstances dictated.

The match had been a dour affair for long periods as Everton hustled Leeds at every opportunity and chances were thin on the ground, nevertheless Everton should have been

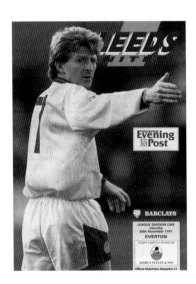

ahead. John Lukic denied them with one stunning save, but Peter Beardsley wasted a couple of glorious openings, the best five minutes from half-time with the goal at his mercy.

Leeds may have failed to overcome tight marking, but the key reason for the dearth of chances was down to referee Tony Ward who continually frustrated home supporters with a number of inconsistent decisions, ruining any chance of a flowing match.

Their patience was finally extinguished when Fairclough was sent off following a clash with Mark Ward; Everton's player only received a caution after he lashed out at the Leeds defender. Reduced to ten men and playing poorly, Howard Wilkinson sent John McClelland on to shore up his defence, sacrificing Steve Hodge, who had been on the field for only six minutes himself.

Clearly angry and shocked at what they saw as an injustice, Leeds players steeled themselves and to their immense credit played the best football of the match. Displaying renewed vigour they got their reward on 83 minutes when Wallace

Leeds United 1
Wallace

Everton 0

SUPER STRIKE! Rod Wallace scores a spectacular winner against Everton.

acrobatically converted a difficult chance following Gordon Strachan's cross that Neville Southall had been unable to claim. It may have been harsh on Everton who had been in control of the match until the dismissal, and arguably deserved a point, but Leeds' resilience in adversity had to be admired.

Referee: T. Ward (London)

Howard Wilkinson, *Yorkshire Evening Post*: 'It seemed innocuous to me. Fairclough fouled Ward, who retaliated, and Fairclough reacted to that. Players are indicted and dealt with by virtue of video evidence so it seems to me that players should be allowed to use the same, that is only natural justice. Everton caused us problems but I was delighted at the spirit we showed. We are scoring goals and winning matches later than we did, and that shows our strength of character.'

Chris Fairclough, *Yorkshire Evening Post*: 'I fouled Ward, he kicked out and I pushed him back down again with the palm of my hand because I sensed there might be confrontation, but I didn't kick him. I wondered if the referee thought I was Chris Whyte, who had been booked earlier, because the first thing he said to me when he came over was that he was going to send me off.'

Referee Tony Ward, *Yorkshire Evening Post*: 'I sent him (Fairclough) off for violent conduct – kicking an opponent. Ward was booked for ungentlemanly conduct.'

Leeds United: Lukic, Sterland, Dorigo, Batty, Fairclough, Whyte, Strachan, Wallace, Chapman, McAllister, Speed (Hodge 65, replaced by McClelland 72)
Everton: Southall, Jackson, Harper, Ebbrell, Watson, Keown, Ward (Warzycha 83), Beardsley, Atteveld, Cottee, Beagrie

LUTON TOWN v. LEEDS UNITED

7 December 1991   Football League, First Division
Kenilworth Road, Luton   Attendance: 11,550

Hot on the heels of their win over Everton, the two teams clashed again at Goodison Park in the Rumbelows Cup (League Cup). Again Leeds came out on top to reach the quarter-finals of the competition for a second successive season. Wilkinson soon banished all talk of cup glory as his side prepared to face Luton Town. Leeds may have suffered only one league defeat in 18 matches but their manager was taking nothing for granted.

Speaking in the *Yorkshire Evening Post* he said, 'Luton may be bottom, but they have only lost twice at home and they are not the worst team in the First Division by a million miles. We are up where the pace is, and when you are in that position if you make a mistake or a wrong decision, others are there to take full advantage. We have to guard against that, if possible.'

TWO QUICK-FIRE GOALS from Rod Wallace and Gary Speed 20 minutes from time settled this clash. With each game the title race is developing into a two-horse race between Leeds and Manchester United, with just one point separating the Pennine rivals.

Leeds' first victory for 32 years at Kenilworth Road took them to 42 points, two ahead of their manager's Christmas target, 10 ahead of third placed Sheffield Wednesday and 13 clear of defending Champions Arsenal.

Luton boss David Pleat promised his team would battle hard and true to his word they fought like tigers against their lofty opponents. The first half in particular was an even affair. Gary McAllister and David Batty fizzed a couple of long-range efforts just over, but the home side came closest to scoring when John Lukic got fingertips to an effort from experienced forward Mick Harford on the half-hour mark.

Slowly but surely though, Leeds began to get a grip on the game after the interval. With McAllister and Gordon Strachan probing for openings and the defence looking solid, a United goal seemed inevitable. That it took until the 69th minute to come is to Luton's credit but the pressure did eventually tell.

The man to break the deadlock was Wallace, with his seventh goal of the season and sixth in five games, as his rich vein of form continued. Wallace's clinical strike from eight yards, after being set up by Lee Chapman, showed his current confidence in front of goal. It was only a half chance but his emphatic finish was that of a man on the top of his game.

The goal galvanised Leeds and within sixty seconds the contest was over when Speed finished off a crisp move with a neat shot.

Referee: P. Vanes (Warley)

Luton Town 0   **Leeds United 2**
                                Wallace
                                Speed

GOOD HATTER! Gary Speed clears the danger from a Luton attack.

David Batty, *Yorkshire Evening Post*: 'If we can keep it going up to Christmas we would have to fancy our chances. We've got the winning habit and when you've got that it often doesn't matter who you are playing. We had to work hard for the result, but that is always to be expected. Winning at home and making sure you don't lose away has always been the key for successful teams. That is the way we are approaching it.'

	P	W	D	L	F	A	Pts
Leeds United	19	12	6	1	34	13	42
Manchester United	18	12	5	1	32	9	41
Sheffield Wed	19	9	5	5	32	22	32
Manchester City	19	9	4	6	25	22	31

Luton Town: Sutton, James (Preece 78), Harvey, Kamara, Dreyer, Peake, Telfer, Stein (Campbell 73), Harford, Pembridge, Oakes

Leeds United: Lukic, Sterland, Dorigo, Batty, Fairclough, Whyte, Strachan, Wallace, Chapman, McAllister, Speed

LEEDS UNITED v. TOTTENHAM HOTSPUR

14 December 1991
Elland Road, Leeds

Football League, First Division
Attendance: 31,404

Only one topic dominated headlines, the double cup draw that had pitted Leeds and Manchester United together in both the Worthington Cup and FA Cup. With a league clash scheduled to take place between the two ties, the teams would go head-to-head in all three competitions at Elland Road at the turn of the New Year. Neither manager could quite believe the trilogy of fixtures, which would generate an estimated £1.12 million in receipts.

Howard Wilkinson, *Yorkshire Evening Post*: 'When you consider what the chances are of this happening it is an unbelievable coincidence. I don't know what the odds would be, if indeed you could have got any, but if you did and this happened you would have broken the bank at Monte Carlo.'

Alex Ferguson, *Yorkshire Evening Post*: 'It is incredible. You are not too surprised to be facing Leeds in the Rumbelows Cup when it is down to the last eight clubs, but for it to happen again in the FA Cup was quite unbelievable.'

As administrators organised tickets for the clashes, Wilkinson turned his thoughts to the Tottenham clash. Speaking with the *Yorkshire Evening Post* he commented, 'We have to forget Manchester United, forget all the hype there has been, forget the fact that all the games are being televised live, and forget what the games mean. A lot of troubled water has to flow under the bridge. We are nearly halfway round the Grand National course, and we all know what can happen in the Grand National.

'Spurs have good players all through the side, and they can come to somewhere like Leeds and before you know what has happened, it is crash, bang, wallop. They can pounce on a mistake, or develop a liking for the atmosphere and suddenly they are playing pretty music. You look at their players on a piece of paper and wonder why they are not top of the League.'

LEEDS RECOVERED from conceding an early goal to claim a deserved point from this exciting encounter thanks to Gary Speed's goal, but the result saw them drop down to second place after Manchester United defeated Chelsea.

The game began badly for Leeds, as Tottenham, clearly fancying their chances of creating an upset, set about their opponents with direct tactics. Gordon Durie and Paul Walsh looked dangerous, and it seemed only a matter of time before a defensive lapse would be punished, and so it proved after 18 minutes when Chris Whyte lost possession near the corner flag to Paul Allen. With midfield players in support, Allen's cross looped off David Howells boot into the net, despite a frantic attempt by Mel Sterland to clear the danger. It was no more than Tottenham deserved for their positive approach.

Leeds regrouped and battled their way back into the match. Rod Wallace went close with a shot, before Erik Thorstvedt saved bravely from the in-form striker, a clash, which the 'keeper later discovered, had broken his nose. Moments later it was Gary McAllister's turn to go close with a superb 30-yard drive that Thorstvedt only just managed to claw away. The pressure was mounting though, and from a Gordon Strachan corner on 38 minutes Leeds equalised when Thorstvedt failed

---

Leeds United 1
Speed

Tottenham 1
Howles

GENTLY DOES IT! Erik Thorstvedt denies Lee Chapman and an acrobatic Gary Speed.

to gather the ball cleanly. Whyte stabbed at the ball, but his shot ricocheted to Speed who swept the ball home.

The second half was a stirring affair, with both teams creating ample opportunities to claim the points. Leeds had 28 (nine on target), Tottenham 14 (7 on target). John Lukic was in fine form, denying Durie and Walsh again with excellent stops, but Thorstvedt was somewhat luckier as Leeds twice struck the woodwork. Whyte was the first to bemoan his luck when he hit a post, before Wallace met David Batty's cross perfectly nine minutes from time, only for his header to loop over the stranded 'keeper and strike the bar. Clearly it was not going to be Leeds' day.

Referee: M. Peck (Kendal)

Howard Wilkinson, *Yorkshire Evening Post*: 'We woke up after the first 15 minutes or so and played very well and produced a game where a 4-3 scoreline would not have been out of place. Suspensions and injuries are becoming a problem. Injuries are part and parcel of the game, but suspensions you can do without. Not only are they a nuisance, they can turn out to be disastrous.'

Leeds United: Lukic, Sterland, Dorigo, Batty, McClelland, Whyte, Strachan, Wallace, Chapman, McAllister, Speed

Tottenham Hotspur: Thorstvedt, Fenwick, Van den Hauwe, Bergsson, Howells, Mabbutt, Stewart, Durie (Sedgley 85), Samways (Nayim 99), Walsh, Allen

Nottingham Forest v. Leeds United

22 December 1991
City Ground, Nottingham

Football League, First Division
Attendance: 27,170

Leeds' popularity on television was extended beyond their trilogy of clashes with Manchester United when ITV announced the league clash at Sheffield Wednesday would be featured on *The Match*. With the Christmas fixtures approaching, Forest and Leeds agreed to delay the game 24 hours to allow supporters the opportunity of enjoying some last-minute shopping for the festivities.

Looking ahead to the match in the *Yorkshire Evening Post*, Howard Wilkinson discussed his team's recent defensive record of five clean sheets in nine games, with just four goals conceded. 'I think a lot is due to the way we play when we have the ball. If you do not give it away as frequently as you might do, it is difficult for the other side to score.'

THIS WAS A DAY when tactical awareness almost brought its just rewards, but Leeds had to settle for a second successive draw following a resolute performance. With Manchester United's game against Aston Villa postponed due to a waterlogged pitch, the point gained took them level at the top, but having played two games more.

Leeds enjoyed a lot of possession, with David Batty playing a deep role in front of his central defenders, but were unable to profit in terms of goals, despite some inspirational moments from Gary McAllister and Gordon Strachan. Batty had an outstanding match, time and again snuffing out Forest raids, to such an extent that they could only muster two worthwhile shots all game. He was also the instigator of numerous Leeds attacks, although the forwards failed to breach the Forest rearguard.

As the game entered the last few minutes, Forest threatened to snatch a winner through Nigel

Clough and substitute Lee Glover, however Leeds' defence held firm. On a day when defences excelled, there was little to choose between Forest's Des Walker and United's Chris Whyte; both were impeccable. It may have only been a point gained, but once again in difficult circumstances the Leeds back line continued to impress.

John McClelland has been in and out of the side in Chris Fairclough's absence but when asked to step in has performed with assurance and has developed a tremendous understanding alongside Whyte, who has grown in stature throughout the season. With Mel Sterland and Tony Dorigo adept at tracking back from their frequent raids forward, Leeds has one of the most flexible defensive line-ups in the division and it paid dividends as the campaign entered the business end of the season.

Referee: M. Reed (Birmingham)

Nottingham Forest 0   Leeds United 0

PACEMAKER! Tony Dorigo storms past Kingsley Black with Gary Speed in support.

Howard Wilkinson, *Yorkshire Evening Post*: 'Our approach was more considered. We never looked like losing the game, but with a 0-0 scoreline you know that you can lose it, but we were pleased with everything, if perhaps a little disappointed that we did not punish Forest more. I thought there was a goal in what we did, and with a little bit of luck we would have been on our way.

'As for David Batty, considering his age and the job he was asked to do, I thought he was exceptional. David showed great discipline. He was a problem to Forest defensively and a problem to them attacking-wise because he had so much of the ball, and started so many of our moves.'

	P	W	D	L	F	A	Pts
Manchester United	19	13	5	1	35	10	44
Leeds United	21	12	8	1	35	14	44
Sheffield Wed	20	10	5	5	34	22	35
Liverpool	20	8	9	3	24	17	33

Nottingham Forest: Crossley, Charles, Pearce, Walker, Tiler, Keane, Black (Glover), Gemmill, Clough, Sheringham, Woan

Leeds United: Lukic, Sterland, Dorigo, Batty, McClelland, Whyte, Strachan (Kelly 73), Wallace, Chapman, McAllister, Speed

Leeds United v. Southampton

26 December 2001
Elland Road, Leeds

Football League, First Division
Attendance: 29,053

There was precious little time to prepare for this Boxing Day clash and pressure was mounting on Leeds to get back on track after dropping four points in the last two games. Leeds faced a Southampton team that had accumulated 41 bookings and three dismissals. The worst offender was centre-half Neil Ruddock with nine bookings and two dismissals; the first had come in the Saints' 4-0 home defeat to Leeds earlier in the season.

Speaking in the *Yorkshire Evening Post,* Howard Wilkinson said: 'When the division is so tight that two league defeats could cost you the title, every point is vital. We have come through half a season, lost only one game while accumulating 43 points, and apart from the last couple of years, under normal circumstances, that would have put us out on our own on top of the First Division. To have played 21 league games and lost only once, as we have this time, is in itself an achievement. They (Southampton) have got disciplinary problems, which no doubt, will have an effect on their performances over the season. As far as we are concerned we have got to go into the game to win it, thereby picking up three points while hoping that we come through without injuries. It is likely to be a tough game.'

DEFENSIVE BLUNDERS cost Leeds dearly despite a brace from Steve Hodge, on a day when the team threw away two points after twice surrendering a two-goal advantage. With Manchester United thumping Oldham Athletic 6-3, the league leaders are now two points clear with two games in hand.

There could be no excuses offered for this dismal result. A title contender with aspirations of a first championship in 18 seasons, and having the second-best record in terms of goals conceded, should have won this match, especially at home, after twice building a comprehensive lead.

Without their injured skipper, Hodge deputised and once again demonstrated his goal-poaching prowess with two goals from close range, both coming from Mel Sterland crosses after 26 and 29 minutes. His fleeting appearances have yielded seven goals in just nine games and it should have been the springboard to success.

In terms of possession and creativity there seemed little danger of Southampton making a fight of it, but five minutes into the second half the game changed when Ian Dowie clinically finished off a six-man move. Suddenly, Leeds appeared vulnerable. Defending deep, they lacked inspiration, but just when they needed a lift Gary Speed settled everyone's nerves with a powerful header from another Sterland cross after 63 minutes.

In normal circumstances this would have been the signal to record a comfortable win, but once again Leeds retreated and eighteen-year-old Alan Shearer began to impose himself against the more experienced John McClelland and Chris Whyte. Strong and direct, it is easy to see why pundits rate the England B international, who justified his growing reputation with a thunderous 30-yard drive after 79 minutes. Southampton was now in the ascendancy, and with Leeds on the back-foot, deservedly grabbed a share of the points with a scrambled goal from the bustling Dowie a minute from time.

Defensively this was a shocker and so unlike performances throughout the first half of the campaign. Hopefully there will be a different Leeds in three days when Manchester United come to town.

Leeds United 3
Hodge (2)
Speed

Southampton 3
Dowie (2)
Shearer

STRETCH! Steve Hodge (above) pokes the ball into the net for one of his brace of goals, before celebrating (below left).

Referee: J. Watson (Whitley Bay)

Howard Wilkinson, *Yorkshire Evening Post:* 'It was the most disappointing performance of my time here. We should have had more than a point, but when you were as disappointing as that you don't deserve more. There were other things about our game that really had nothing to do with ability or talent. There were too many unforced errors, not enough assertiveness from individuals, and we were too content to drift along and tolerate each other when really it needed someone out on the pitch to get angry.'

Southampton: Flowers, Wood, Adams, Hurlock, Gittens, Moore, Horne, Cockerill, Shearer, Dowie, Gray

Leeds United: Lukic, Sterland, Dorigo, Batty, McClelland, Whyte, Hodge, Wallace, Chapman, McAllister, Speed

Leeds United v. Manchester United

29 December 1991
Elland Road, Leeds

Football League, First Division
Attendance: 32,638

Leading into this match the two teams' form could not have contrasted more. Whilst Leeds had picked up three successive draws, Manchester United had collected three wins, scoring 13 goals in the process. Looking forward to a titanic battle, the Leeds manager told the *Yorkshire Evening Post*: 'We won't need any motivating for this game. The players will be as keen as anyone, particularly as the game will be watched by millions of people on television, to get Boxing Day out of their systems. There is still a lot of football to be played in this championship.'

MEL STERLAND'S COOLLY TAKEN PENALTY on 80 minutes earned Leeds a share of the spoils in a thrilling battle between the top two sides in the First Division. This was a much better performance from Leeds after their faltering displays in recent weeks. They matched their Pennine rivals in every department and thoroughly deserved to draw.

It was tense throughout, both sides knew the importance of the occasion, and the first half brought few clear-cut chances but there was plenty of determination, skill, hard tackling and passion to keep supporters and television viewers on the edge of their seats. For Leeds, knowing that a defeat would leave them five points adrift at the top, David Batty was sensational, battling away in defence and the middle of the park, but in attack Lee Chapman and Rod Wallace struggled against the indomitable partnership of Steve Bruce and Gary Pallister. Neil Webb looked dangerous for the Reds, but the pick was Mark Hughes, who, ignoring Leeds fans' jeers, led the line with his usual tenacity.

The match sprung into action in the opening moments of the second half when John Lukic saved well from Ryan Giggs, but no sooner had Leeds cleared their lines than they fell behind to a well-struck shot by Webb from 20 yards. Television replays showed Giggs standing in an offside position and Bruce appeared to pull back Chris Whyte, but the goal stood.

Feeling aggrieved, Leeds battled on but had to survive some close calls as the visitors stepped up the tempo. Nevertheless, they appeared to have pulled themselves back into the match when Chapman converted Batty's cross on 65 minutes. However, referee Mr Bob Nixon controversially awarded Leeds a free kick for an infringement on Batty whilst delivering his cross. Gary McAllister's effort came to nothing and as the minutes ticked by Howard Wilkinson sacrificed Batty for Steve Hodge.

Ten minutes from time Leeds finally got the break their endeavour deserved when Pallister was adjudged to have fouled McAllister for a penalty. Sterland stepped up for the spot kick, in place of Gordon Strachan (struggling with a back injury), and could not have struck the ball more sweetly, wrong-footing Peter Schmeichel for a crucial equaliser. Leeds more than held their own in the remaining minutes to gain a share of the spoils and maintain the status quo.

Referee: B. Nixon (Wirral)

Howard Wilkinson, *Yorkshire Evening Post*: 'It was vital that we didn't lose because we deserved at least a draw out of the game. The teams are very evenly matched. I did feel that we were a little unlucky with the decisions for their goal, because Chris Whyte was impeded and one of their players was offside.

Leeds United 1
Sterland (Penalty)

Manchester United 1
Webb

TOP BOSS! Howard Wilkinson receives the November Manager of the Month award.

We also didn't get the luck when the referee disallowed Lee Chapman's goal, bringing play back for a free kick to us.'

Mel Sterland, *Yorkshire Evening Post*: 'We discussed the situation at half-time and Gordon said that if there was a penalty he felt it better if someone else took it, and I was only too happy to oblige. When the referee pointed to the spot, no one was going to take the ball from me. Sure, there was a lot at stake but I haven't missed a penalty for Leeds yet and I thrive on pressure. We couldn't afford to lose and let Manchester United go five points clear.'

Alex Ferguson, *Yorkshire Evening Post*: 'We got what we deserved. We sat back trying to protect our lead and that's a dangerous thing to do and we paid the penalty, but I hold my hands up to Leeds. There was something almost kamikaze about them. They were buzzing all over the place in the end because they had the policy of just going for it. They took risks, had a real go at us and got a point.'

	P	W	D	L	F	A	Pts
Manchester United	21	14	6	1	42	14	48
Leeds United	23	12	10	1	39	18	46
Sheffield Wed	22	11	6	5	36	23	39
Manchester City	23	11	6	6	32	27	39

Leeds United: Lukic, Sterland, Dorigo, Batty (Hodge 74), Fairclough, Whyte, Strachan, Wallace, Chapman, McAllister, Speed

Manchester United: Schmeichel, Parker, Blackmore (Sharpe 88), Bruce, Webb, Pallister, Kanchelskis (Donaghy 82), Ince, McClair, Hughes, Giggs

NO GOAL! Chapman scores but the referee awards Leeds a free kick for a foul on Batty.

ICE COOL! Mel Sterland takes a crucial penalty against league leaders Manchester United.

ALL SQUARE! Another view of Leeds' crucial equaliser.

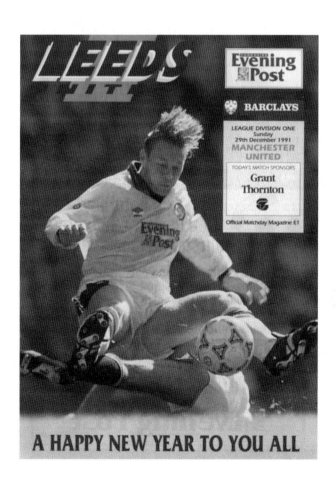

WEST HAM UNITED v. LEEDS UNITED

1 January 1992
Upton Park, London

Football League, First Division
Attendance: 21,766

Leeds travelled south hoping to return to their winning ways against a West Ham team deep in relegation trouble and determined to end their own poor run of form, having lost five of their previous six matches.

Leeds 'keeper John Lukic told the *Yorkshire Evening Post*: 'We cannot afford to take a breather now and must be as professional as we were against Manchester United. West Ham are desperate for points, just as we are, and we cannot afford to take things lightly.'

Leeds boss Howard Wilkinson added, 'Consistency is vital in such a long and difficult season. Good teams do not allow their heads to be turned by short-term glory. They face the times of adversity and summon the reserves of inner belief to conquer the challenges in their way.'

TWO GOALS FROM LEE CHAPMAN took him into double figures for the season as Leeds got back on the winning trail. The victory sent them back to the top of the table with Manchester United surprisingly losing 4-1 at home to QPR.

This was a must win game for Leeds after four successive draws and they got off to a flyer from Chapman on 11 minutes. The goal arrived following an exchange of passes between Gordon Strachan and Gary McAllister, who had forced a sharp save from Ludek Miklosko moments earlier. This time the cultured Scot played a beautifully weighted cross for Chapman to out-jump two defenders before powering home an unstoppable header from seven yards.

The opening strike was no more than Leeds deserved, and with West Ham capitulating in recent weeks after conceding a goal, they must have been confident of recording a win. However, the Hammers were handed a lifeline when Tony Dorigo held back Kevin Keen in the penalty area. Julian Dicks made no mistake from the spot kick on 24 minutes awarded by referee Ron Groves.

The equalising goal stiffened Leeds' resolve and they regained the lead on the half hour when McAllister accepted a pass from Chapman to fire home a powerful shot. Leeds were in the

ascendancy and nearly extended their advantage before half-time when Gary Speed's shot was hacked off the line.

After the break, West Ham, to their credit, came back into the match and Leeds had to rely on John Lukic to keep their tenuous lead intact. Time and again Lukic rescued his side denying Small, Bishop and Breaker with notable saves. Leeds were still dangerous on the counter attack though, and Strachan should have scored when clean through after 65 minutes, but in the end it was left to Chapman to clinch the points when he gleefully swept home Rod Wallace's excellent pass five minutes from time.

This may not have been vintage Leeds but the points were welcome, especially with the news from Old Trafford.

Referee: R. Groves (Weston-super-Mare)

West Ham United 1
Dicks (Penalty)

Leeds United 3
Chapman (2)
McAllister

WEST HAM UNITED v. LEEDS UNITED

Above: HAPPY NEW YEAR! Lee Chapman strokes home the opening goal in a fine win.

Right: COOL GUY! Goalscorer Gary McAllister composes himself before striking at goal.

Howard Wilkinson: 'I was very pleased with the result but our performance was not one of our better ones. I don't know really what was missing, and I do not think the players know either, but we were that bad at times we made West Ham look good. But we always managed to stop them at the end, the goalkeeper or the centre backs always did something, though I thought we made the better scoring chances.'

West Ham United: Miklosko, Breacker, Dicks, Gale, Potts, Thomas, Bishop, McAvennie, Small (Morley 69), Keen, Slater

Leeds United: Lukic, Sterland, Dorigo, Batty, Fairclough, Whyte, Strachan, Wallace, Chapman, McAllister, Speed

SHEFFIELD WEDNESDAY v. LEEDS UNITED

12 January 1992   Football League, First Division
Hillsborough, Sheffield   Attendance: 32,228

Leeds' preparations for this vital Yorkshire 'derby' were dented following a 3-1 defeat to Manchester United in the Rumbelows Cup. Howard Wilkinson told the *Yorkshire Evening Post*: 'Strength of character has to be shown now. My players have got to pick themselves up to make sure they get this performance out of their system. They have to show people, and more importantly, themselves that they can deal with defeat as well as victory. We have been at the top or second in the league for all but five or six weeks of the season. That is a long time and represents a lot of effort, sweat, determination and ability. It would be a sad reflection if one defeat and one performance were allowed to jeopardise all that ground work.'

LEE CHAPMAN scored a hat-trick against his old team as Leeds, reclaiming pole position, recorded their biggest away win in over 60 years with a six-goal annihilation of their South Yorkshire neighbours.

Even without Gordon Strachan through injury and the suspended David Batty, Leeds were far too strong in every department for a dispirited and forlorn-looking Wednesday side who could not wait for the final whistle to end this live television extravaganza.

Howard Wilkinson's team, back to their flowing best, seemed capable of scoring at will as they exorcised the disappointment of their cup exit in devastating fashion. Taking control from the kick off, Leeds attacked down the flanks and it didn't take them long to strike when Chapman grabbed the opening goal on eight minutes when he scored from close range after Chris Fairclough headed back Gary McAllister's corner across the face of the goal.

The former Wednesday star nearly added a second when he forced Chris Woods into a smart save before thumping a shot against the bar following a flowing move. Carl Shutt was next to rue a missed chance, before Tony Dorigo crashed an unstoppable free kick from 25 yards into the top corner of the net with a brilliant strike after 33 minutes. Wednesday reduced the deficit in controversial fashion six minutes later when Chris Whyte was adjudged to have fouled Gordon Watson by referee Philip Don for a penalty kick. Leeds' appeals that Watson had dived were backed up by television replays but John Sheridan scored after Lukic had pushed his initial kick onto a post.

Clearly aggrieved, Leeds pushed forward and quickly re-established their two-goal cushion before half-time. Dorigo instigated the opening down the left flank, and combining with Speed, Chapman crashed home the Welshman's pinpoint cross past a defenceless Woods for a sensational goal.

The second half saw Leeds in total control. Woods saved from Wallace, McAllister, Chapman and Steve Hodge, but with the pressure mounting it was only a matter of time before Leeds grabbed their fourth goal, which duly arrived when Chapman completed his hat-trick after Speed's header had come back off the bar after 66 minutes.

Before the end Mike Whitlow grabbed his first goal of the season before Wallace wrapped things up with a sixth, three minutes from time. This was a virtuoso performance from Leeds. The club's biggest away win in the league since 1930 when Blackpool were defeated 7-3, and the Owls heaviest home defeat in their 100-year league history. Wilkinson's team had answered their critics most emphatically that they would last the pace.

Referee: P. Don (Middlesex)

Sheffield Wednesday 1   **Leeds United 6**
   Sheridan   *Chapman 3, Dorigo*
                                            Whitlow, Wallace

Above: FIRST BLOOD! Lee Chapman nets the opening goal.

Right: TREBLE CHANCE! Chapman grabs his third goal and Leeds' fourth of the match.

Sheffield Wednesday: Woods, Nilsson, King, Palmer, Anderson, Pearson (Harkes 46), Watson, Sheridan, Bart-Williams, Jemson, Worthington (Williams 64)

Leeds United: Lukic, Sterland, Dorigo, Hodge (Davison 81), Fairclough, Whyte, Shutt (Whitlow 62), Wallace, Chapman, McAllister, Speed

STARMAN! Chapman receives the congratulations of his team mates.

HAT-TRICK HERO!

DOWN AND OUT! Rod Wallace grabs the sixth goal.

LEEDS UNITED v. CRYSTAL PALACE

18 January 1992
Elland Road, Leeds

Football League, First Division
Attendance: 27,717

Leeds bowed out of the FA Cup prior to this fixture. Fans wondered not only how they would react to this latest defeat to Manchester United, but of more concern, who would replace Lee Chapman in attack after he broke a wrist following an aerial clash with Gary Pallister.

Although disappointed, Howard Wilkinson was not too despondent. 'We played well, created more chances (than in the Rumbelows Cup), but we made one mistake and paid for it. Manchester United were lucky to win but that is cup football and you have to take things like this on the chin. The players have got to mourn our cup exit but then the mourning has got to end, and we will take all the positive stuff out of the game into the next game.'

Wilkinson described Chapman's absence for up to eight weeks as a 'crushing blow' but would consider his options after the Palace match with the club having no game the following week. In Chapman's absence Gary Speed would play as an auxiliary striker.

CHRIS FAIRCLOUGH salvaged a point with his first goal of the season as Leeds dropped two more points in a dour match. The team's frustration was only marginally eased with news that Manchester United had been held at Notts County.

With Gary Speed spearheading the attack, not surprisingly it took Leeds time to settle, but following a placid opening, it was still something of a shock when Palace scored on 17 minutes after Steve Hodge had been penalised for a foul on Gareth Southgate. Chris Whyte appeared to have cleared the initial danger from Andy Gray's free kick but the ball fell nicely for Eagles skipper Geoff Thomas to fire home from 20 yards.

Clearly shaken, Leeds almost went two behind moments later when Mark Bright, looking suspiciously offside, fired wide with only John Lukic to beat. United, urged on by Gordon Strachan, came more into the game and Hodge was unlucky with two efforts that were saved smartly by Eagles 'keeper Nigel Martyn.

Undeterred, Leeds continued to press and deservedly equalised after 32 minutes from Strachan's corner, Speed flicking on for Fairclough to stab home. Two minutes from the break Bobby Davison replaced Gary McAllister, suffering with a groin injury, but it did not impact on Leeds' creativity in the second period as they dominated possession.

For long periods the Londoners were on the defensive as Leeds chased a third consecutive league win, but as in their previous home fixture, luck seemed to be conspiring against them. Twice they struck woodwork, through Speed and Wallace. Clearly this was not going to be their day.

Referee: T. Fitzharris (Bolton)

Howard Wilkinson, *Yorkshire Evening Post*: 'I knew how hard this match would be for us and how important it was. We deserved to win but we did not lose it. But it was not too disappointing because after 20 minutes we picked the game up, got at them and from then on could not have a lot of complaints.'

Leeds United 1
Fairclough

Crystal Palace 1
Thomas

POINT SAVER! Chris Fairclough strikes to earn Leeds a draw.

Gary Speed goes close with this header.

Leeds United: Lukic, Sterland, Dorigo, Batty, Fairclough, Whyte, Strachan, Wallace, Hodge (Whitlow 85), McAllister (Davison 42), Speed
Crystal Palace: Martyn, Humphrey, Sinnott, Gray, Southgate, Thorn, Rodger, Thomas, Bright, Gabbiadini (Whyte 60), McGoldrick

LEEDS UNITED v. NOTTS COUNTY

1 February 1992
Elland Road, Leeds

Football League, First Division
Attendance: 27,224

As Leeds relaxed on their enforced short break, Manchester United took full advantage from the first of their games in hand with a hard-fought 1-0 win over Aston Villa. Now two points ahead with a game in hand, betting odds remained unchanged, Alex Ferguson's team 5:2 on favourites, Leeds 4:1 against. ITV still believed there was plenty to play for, announcing they would be covering United's clash at Everton live on *The Match*.

The result brought little reaction from the Leeds boss, but he did comment on all the strikers he was supposed to be interested in signing, which included Tony Cascarino (Celtic), Steve Bull (Wolves), Brian Deane (Sheffield United), Frank Farina (Bari) and Kalman Kovacs (Auxerre). Speaking in the *Yorkshire Evening Post*, the Leeds boss said, 'People have been quick to make things up and they choose to believe what they hear rather that what I tell them, so we have had a week of headline rumours and half truths. If and when there is anything definite I will say so.'

With no game scheduled for two weeks, and only spasmodic training due to some horrendous weather, Leeds was thankful that Bayern Munich agreed to play a friendly game. Following the 1-1 draw, a match Howard Wilkinson described as 'a good work-out'; the team prepared for their clash with Notts County. With Gary McAllister responding to treatment, Wilkinson had a full squad available.

A CRACKING DRIVE by David Batty, only the third goal of his career, helped Leeds to a comfortable 3-0 win. With Manchester United drawing at Arsenal, Leeds went back to the top by virtue of a better goal difference.

Following an undistinguished opening to this match, Leeds opened the scoring after 12 minutes when Mel Sterland headed home Gordon Strachan's corner from close range for his seventh goal of the season, and 70th of his career. The visitors responded with a shot by Kevin Bartlett but John Lukic saved comfortably. Tommy Johnson also went close, but Leeds had the greater possession and Gary Speed was agonisingly wide with an angled drive. County 'keeper Steve Cherry had to

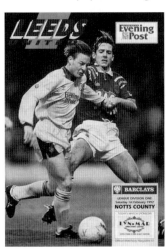

be on his toes when Alan Paris, under pressure from Chris Fairclough, almost scored an own goal. Overall though, Leeds struggled to break through a dogged defence.

In the second half Mike Whitlow replaced Sterland, the Leeds full back not having recovered from an ankle injury sustained just before the break. Whitlow was soon called upon when he made a crucial interception to deny Bartlett, before Leeds doubled their advantage with a sensational solo goal from Batty. The goal followed a County corner, which Tony Dorigo cleared to the Leeds midfielder. Setting off on a determined 60-yard run from inside his own half, Batty shrugged off a challenge from Dean Thomas before cutting infield towards County's goal. Although he had players in support, Batty was going it alone and unleashed a thunderous rising shot past a despairing Cherry from just inside the penalty area for his second goal of the season.

Rod Wallace set the seal on a comfortable win 13 minutes from time with a deflected shot after Steve Hodge had knocked back a

---

Leeds United 3
Sterland, Batty
Wallace

Notts County 0

TOP SHOT! David Batty runs to the Kop after putting his side 2-0 ahead.

Strachan cross. The final score may have flattered Leeds, but they will have been thankful for a first home win since November.

Referee: D. Allison (Lancaster)

Howard Wilkinson, *Yorkshire Evening Post*: 'We were not at our best but credit to County for, maybe, not allowing us to show ourselves in our best light. We had to scrap and fight for it but it was a great result and ample proof that if you keep at it, the luck comes good. There are no bad goals but the one David got against Notts County was terrific … a hell of a goal.'

	P	W	D	L	F	A	Pts
Leeds United	27	15	11	1	52	21	56
Manchester United	26	16	8	2	47	20	56
Liverpool	27	12	11	4	35	24	47
Manchester City	27	13	8	6	36	29	47

Leeds United: Lukic, Sterland (Whitlow 46), Dorigo, Batty, Fairclough, Whyte, Strachan (Kelly 80), Wallace, Hodge, McAllister, Speed
Notts County: Cherry, Palmer, Paris, Short, Dryden (Wells 68), Draper, Thomas, Turner, Lund, Bartlett, Johnson (Slawson 60)

OLDHAM ATHLETIC v. LEEDS UNITED

8 February 1992
Boundary Park, Oldham

Football League, First Division
Attendance: 18,409

As this fixture approached, one story dominated headlines … the signing of Nimes and French international striker Eric Cantona as Howard Wilkinson boosted his options with the continued absence of Lee Chapman. Signed initially on a £100,000 loan deal until mid-April, a further £900,000 would make Cantona's transfer permanent.

Cantona had been on trial at Sheffield Wednesday, but when the move hit snags, Wilkinson nipped in. Seen as the biggest gamble of his managerial career, Wilkinson said in a *Yorkshire Evening Post* interview: 'I have not signed a player before in these circumstances but I have seen him play on video and spoken about him with people such as Michel Platini and Glenn Hoddle. They all said, without reservation, there is no problem with the boy and that his ability is not in doubt. He is passionate about his football and he has got a wide view of life. Obviously he has come to one of the best teams in the country so will have a fight on his hands to get into the side. He is a player of exceptional quality and for a big lad he has a terrific touch, good vision and an ability to bring other people into the game.'

Speaking through an interpreter Cantona told local reporters, 'The problems I have had have been little ones that have been exaggerated. I have been training on my own and it has gone very well. I feel quite fit and I will train as hard as I can this week in the hope of getting into the Leeds side and then it will be down to the manager whether he picks me or not.' On the eve of the match, Wilkinson confirmed Cantona would play some part.

Prior to the match the club was informed about two fixture changes. For the second time in three weeks they would have a blank weekend due to Aston Villa's involvement in the FA Cup. Two friendly matches were quickly set up against Shelbourne and IFK Gothenberg. Regarding their derby clash at Sheffield United on 25 April, it would now be played 24 hours later at police request (12.00 noon).

TWO GOALS SENT LEEDS CRASHING to their second league defeat of the season. Only once in 14 attempts since the 1927/28 season have Leeds departed from Boundary Park with a win, so it was not too surprising to leave empty-handed as Manchester United returned to the top.

Leeds for long periods were outfought by a battling display from Joe Royle's team who took a grip on the game after 18 minutes when Paul Bernard fired home from close range after Richard Jobson's header had struck a post following a flick-on from Rick Holden's corner. The winger was a thorn in Leeds' side throughout the match and was unlucky not to double his side's lead when he struck a post with a terrific 20-yard free-kick just after the half hour mark.

Just before the interval Rod Wallace hit the bar with a fine strike, but the linesman had already signalled for offside, and Leeds' luck was out once more when the referee turned down appeals for a penalty after Mel Sterland was bundled over by Ian Marshall.

Eric Cantona came on for his Leeds debut at the start of the second half when Steve Hodge departed with a calf injury, but his

---

Oldham Athletic 2
  Bernard
  Barlow

Leeds United 0

FRENCH CONNECTION! Eric Cantona tries his luck on his Leeds debut.

only opportunity came when Gordon Strachan sent him clear following a quick throw in. Unfortunately for the Frenchman, Andy Barlow stopped his run into the Oldham penalty area.

Leeds battled hard to find an equaliser, but only managed one weak header from Cantona. Two minutes from time, Oldham settled the match when Barlow fired home Holden's centre.

Referee: A. Wilkie (Chester-le-Street)

Howard Wilkinson, *Yorkshire Evening Post*: 'They did not allow us a kick. I have been here three times now with Leeds and we have hardly had a kick in any of the games. Even when we beat them at our place we were lucky.'

	P	W	D	L	F	A	Pts
Manchester United	27	16	9	2	48	21	57
Leeds United	28	15	11	2	52	23	56
Liverpool	28	12	12	4	35	24	48
Sheffield Wed	27	13	8	6	43	33	47

Oldham Athletic: Hallworth, Barrett, Barlow, Henry, Jobson, Marshall, Palmer, Bernard, Sharp, McDonald, Holden

Leeds United: Lukic, Sterland (Whitlow 79), Dorigo, Batty, Fairclough, Whyte, Strachan, Wallace, Hodge (Cantona 45), McAllister, Speed

EVERTON v. LEEDS UNITED

23 February 1992
Goodison Park, Liverpool

Football League, First Division
Attendance: 19,248

Due to international matches, preparations were severely hampered but Howard Wilkinson was satisfied with his team's efforts in friendly games against Shelbourne (2-0) and IFK Gothenberg (0-1). With everyone reporting back fit, the Leeds boss had a full squad to choose from, apart from Lee Chapman.

LEEDS' TITLE AMBITIONS were dealt a blow when they threw away two vital points after taking the lead from a Martin Keown own goal. The draw handed the initiative to Manchester United, now three points clear having played one match less following their latest win.

This was a poor game, with few clear-cut chances and a game dominated by defences. Gordon Strachan, David Batty and Gary McAllister battled away in midfield, but all too often they failed to find the killer pass. With Eric Cantona making his full debut, there was great expectation from United supporters. The Frenchman had a quiet game, but did create one opening out of nothing. Picking the ball up in the centre circle he galloped past Dave Watson into the penalty box. The angle needed an instinctive left-foot strike, but switching to his right, he pulled the opportunity wide of the far post.

Overall the first half was a frenzied affair, with only one flash of inspiration 10 minutes before the break when Rod Wallace teed up an opportunity for McAllister from Strachan's cross. The Scot's 30-yard shot was superb, as was Neville Southall's save.

During the interval Carl Shutt replaced Wallace, who had a nasty shin injury, and soon became the hero following a defensive mix-up between Everton goalkeeper Southall and Watson. Presented with an opening Shutt played a dangerous cross along the goal line, which was turned into his own net by the unfortunate Keown on 58 minutes. Everton boss Howard Kendall immediately brought Peter Beagrie and Andy Hinchcliffe into the fray, and within eight minutes Beagrie's accurate corner was flicked on by Gary Ablett to Matthew Jackson for the simplest of chances to equalise at the far post. The set piece was well worked, but Leeds' marking was non-existent.

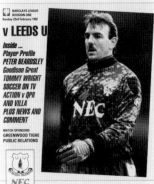

This was a lacklustre performance for the second match running by Leeds, but the Leeds boss would have been encouraged by his defence who were outstanding apart from one lapse of concentration.

Referee: B. Hill (Kettering)

Howard Wilkinson, *Yorkshire Evening Post*: 'We are just marginally the second-best team in the country at the moment and that's across all four leagues. We mustn't let one disappointment lead to the next. We are in the home straight now just behind the front-runners. The pace was always going to pick up and we have got to stay the course. No one is kidding themselves that the Everton match was the best performance in the world, but we got a point when we could have ended up with nothing.'

Everton 1	Leeds United 1
Jackson	*Keown (Own Goal)*

COLLISION COURSE! Martin Keown (marking Eric Cantona) is seconds away from turning Carl Shutt's cross into his own net.

	P	W	D	L	F	A	Pts
Manchester United	28	17	9	2	50	21	60
Leeds United	29	15	12	2	53	24	57
Manchester City	30	14	8	8	43	35	50
Sheffield Wed	29	14	8	7	46	41	50

Everton: Southall, Jackson, Ablett, Ebbrell, Watson, Keown, Warzycha (Beagrie 58), Beardsley, Johnston, Cottee (Hinchcliffe 58), Ward
Leeds United: Lukic, Sterland, Dorigo, Batty, Fairclough, Whyte, Strachan, Wallace (Shutt 46), Cantona, McAllister, Speed

LEEDS UNITED v. LUTON TOWN

29 February 1992   Football League, First Division
Elland Road, Leeds   Attendance: 28,231

The biggest concern for Leeds during the week was their mounting injuries, Rod Wallace being the latest victim with a shin injury. Fortunately, X-rays revealed only bruising. With his chances of facing Luton more positive, as were Lee Chapman's following a visit to the specialist, the focus was turning ever more intently on Eric Cantona, who had failed to make an immediate impression in his opening appearances. Although it was early days, he was keen to overcome his disappointing introduction to First Division football.

There was relief for Leeds when Manchester United failed to defeat Chelsea in their remaining match in hand, but their 1-1 gave them a four-point advantage. The pressure to eat into their advantage was firmly on the Yorkshire side. On the eve of the Luton clash, Wilkinson, concerned about cover for his strikers, agreed a one-month exchange deal with Notts County for Tony Agana, with veteran defender John McClelland going in the other direction.

ERIC CANTONA'S FIRST GOAL in English football set Leeds on the road to a 2-0 win against struggling Luton Town but this was an unconvincing performance by the title chasers. Nevertheless, Leeds reduced the deficit at the top of table to just two points following Manchester United's 0-0 draw at Coventry City.

With Rod Wallace and Lee Chapman named in the side, expectations were high for a comfortable win. The match began brightly with Tony Dorigo in particular prominent on the left flank, but Dorigo had to leave the field when he twisted his knee on 29 minutes. Gary Speed switched to left-back as Cantona entered the fray, but with ex-Leeds midfielder Chris Kamara, who was given a rapturous applause on his return, making life difficult for David Batty and Gary McAllister, Leeds struggled to find any rhythm.

Defensive uncertainty by Chris Fairclough and Chris Whyte gave Gary Penbridge a couple of glorious opportunities, but Leeds survived and they were unlucky not to take a first-half lead when Whtye had an effort blocked on the line and Fairclough clipped the crossbar.

When Cantona, cheered at his every touch, blazed over from close range early in the second half, he shook his head in disbelief. Supporters wondered if it was going to be one of those

frustrating days, especially after Wallace waltzed past three defenders only to see his effort strike the bar. To Leeds' credit though they battled on and got their reward after 58 minutes through Cantona. McAllister created the opening with a surging run into the Luton penalty area, only to be brought down by 'keeper Steve Sutton. The referee allowed advantage for Cantona to thump the ball home.

At last Leeds looked in control although Mick Harford and Brian Stein squandered a couple of openings. Five minutes from time Leeds finally wrapped up the points when Lee Chapman marked his return to the side with a thumping drive after being set up by Cantona's neat header. It was a stuttering display by the home side, and the Leeds boss was clearly a relieved manager at the end, but the title race is interestingly poised.

Referee: A. Flood (Stockport)

Leeds United 2   **Luton Town 0**
Cantona
Chapman

BACK WITH A BANG! Lee Chapman is about to mark his return with a stunning goal.

Howard Wilkinson, *Yorkshire Evening Post*: 'I did not need any convincing about his (Cantona's) ability, but he's finding out what life here is all about very quickly.'

	P	W	D	L	F	A	Pts
Manchester United	30	17	11	2	51	22	62
Leeds United	30	16	12	2	55	24	60
Manchester City	31	15	8	8	45	35	53
Sheffield Wed	30	15	8	7	49	41	53

Leeds United: Lukic, Sterland, Dorigo (Cantona 29), Batty, Fairclough, Whyte, Strachan, Wallace (Agana 81), Chapman, McAllister, Speed

Luton Town: Sutton, James, Harvey, Kamara, Dreyer, Peake, Hughes (Salton 84), Campbell (Stein 74), Harford, Pembridge, Preece

LEEDS UNITED v. ASTON VILLA

3 March 1992
Elland Road, Leeds

Football League, First Division
Attendance: 28,896

Back in title contention, Leeds had an opportunity to reclaim pole position with a second successive home win. Apart from the left-back position, Howard Wilkinson's only selection dilemma was if Eric Cantona would stay in the side after his first goal for the club or whether new signing Tony Agana would make his debut.

Speaking in the *Yorkshire Evening Post*, Villa manager Ron Atkinson said, 'It will be a cauldron at Elland Road. A few weeks ago I thought Manchester United were favourites but now Leeds have come bouncing back.' Wilkinson commented, 'Once you get to this stage in the championship race when there are only 12 games left, the prize becomes bigger than the teams you are playing against.'

A PENALTY MISS by Gordon Strachan in the second half proved costly as Leeds failed to win a seventh league match at home this season. Howard Wilkinson's team may be only a point adrift of leaders Manchester United, who have a game in hand, but the biggest headache for the Leeds boss is the number of players being added to the club's injury list.

There was plenty to ponder for supporters before kick-off with Mike Whitlow replacing Tony Dorigo and Tony Agana being preferred to Eric Cantona, after Rod Wallace was rested, but nobody could have predicted the bizarre start the match would have. Leeds began brightly with Agana going close after three minutes, but barely sixty seconds later Mel Sterland and Chris Fairclough clashed heads when challenging for an aerial ball with Cyril Regis. Following a lengthy delay both left the pitch for further treatment.

Play was not surprisingly disjointed, but to Leeds' credit they ensured that Villa was unable to prosper from their numerical advantage. Both players returned, Sterland with six stitches to a head wound, but Fairclough soon departed with a nasty eye injury just past the half-hour mark. John McLelland (prior to his loan move) entered the fray and immediately settled, making some timely interceptions.

Agana almost broke the deadlock with a header that struck the top of the bar, but after 57 minutes Leeds should have taken the lead when they were awarded a penalty. Unfortunately,

Gordon Strachan spurned the chance with a weak shot that was easily saved by Nigel Spink. It was only the Leeds skipper's third miss in 21 attempts for the team, but it did not affect his play as he urged greater effort.

Cantona replaced Agana after 65 minutes and immediately added a spark to the attack. Forcing nine corners in the last 15 minutes, compared to just two before, Leeds piled on the pressure, but the closest they came to a goal were two strikes by the Frenchman, which were well saved by Spink.

A disappointing result maybe, but the opening minutes of this clash stacked the odds against Leeds. Both Sterland and Fairclough were detained in hospital overnight, before being released the following morning.

Referee: P. Wright (Norwich)

Leeds United 0   Aston Villa 0

NO ENTRY! Speed, Agana and Strachan struggle to get past Paul McGrath and Earl Barrett.

Howard Wilkinson, *Yorkshire Evening Post*: 'We could hardly have had a worse start. The injuries we suffered had a disrupting influence on us but we managed to get a bit of steam up later on, which is what you would expect from a team going for the prize we are aiming for. There are no easy football matches and half a loaf is better than none so you just have to keep on going. The more penalties you have to take the more likelihood that you are going to miss the odd one or two. Gordon maybe didn't strike the ball as well as he could, and the goalkeeper guessed the right way, but penalty taking is a bit like roulette.'

	P	W	D	L	F	A	Pts
Manchester United	30	17	11	2	51	22	62
Leeds United	31	16	13	2	55	24	61
Manchester City	31	15	8	8	45	35	53
Sheffield Wed	30	15	8	7	49	41	53

Leeds United: Lukic, Sterland, Whitlow, Batty, Fairclough (McClelland 36), Whyte, Strachan, Agana (Cantona 65), Chapman, McAllister, Speed

Aston Villa: Spink, Barrett, Staunton, Teale, McGrath, Richardson, Daley, Parker, Regis, Atkinson, Blake

Tottenham Hotspur v. Leeds United

7 March 1992
White Hart Lane, London

Football League, First Division
Attendance: 27,622

With the return of Rod Wallace to the first-team squad, in addition to Mel Sterland and Chris Fairclough reporting fit, the main decision for Leeds manager Howard Wilkinson was who to play in attack alongside Lee Chapman. With Eric Cantona, Tony Agana and the returning Wallace to select from it was an interesting choice for the Leeds boss, but his more immediate concern was to guard against complacency when playing against a team that had the worst home defensive record in the league.

Speaking in the *Yorkshire Evening Post* prior to the team's departure to London, he said, 'We know of Tottenham's home record and it frightens me to death! The longer a team goes on winning the more likely it is they will lose, and by the same token the longer a team goes on losing the more likely it is they will win a game. But, at this stage of the campaign it doesn't matter which team we are playing. It is simply a case of worrying about matches not teams.'

TWO GOALS in as many minutes from substitute Jon Newsome, and Gary McAllister, brought Leeds three more points in their quest for the championship. Moving two points clear at the top, this was an important win after dropping two points in their last encounter, although their Pennine rivals had two games in hand.

Leeds began brightly, but Tottenham had early opportunities through Gordon Durie. The Scot was thwarted by John Lukic after 10 minutes, but should have opened the scoring shortly after when clean through. Fortunately for the visitors his hesitancy allowed Lukic to gather the ball just in time. On the half hour he was again bemoaning his luck when Lukic made another sharp save.

Leeds made Tottenham pay dearly six minutes later when Rod Wallace, who had been preferred to partner Lee Chapman in attack, justified his selection when he clinically struck home David Batty's astute pass. On the balance of play it was harsh on Tottenham, but they were soon back in the match after the resumption of play when Paul Allen finished off a superb pass by the impressive Paul Stewart.

With the game in the balance, Howard Wilkinson replaced Mel Sterland with Jon Newsome for only his second appearance of the season, and the twenty-one-year-old summer signing instantly became a hero when he thundered home an unstoppable header on 76 minutes from Gordon Strachan's corner.

Sensing victory, Wilkinson brought Eric Cantona on in place of Mike Whitlow, switching Gary Speed to left-back. Within a minute the Frenchman had sent McAllister clear with a superb pass, the Scot finishing with aplomb to settle any lingering nerves that had developed among both players and supporters. This was a confidence-boosting victory for Leeds who could be well pleased with their professional efficiency.

Referee: R. Gifford (Glamorgan)

Tottenham Hotspur 1
Allen

Leeds United 3
Wallace, Newsome, McAllister

OPENER! Rod Wallace races through to blast Leeds ahead.

Howard Wilkinson: 'It was a great result but not our best performance. We showed a lot of character because the game was not giving us much and we were not playing well. We hung in there and won through in the end. The full backs were marvellous and the goalkeeper was terrific. He kept us in it at times.'

Jon Newsome added: 'With 20 minutes of the game left the gaffer just said to me get on and make a name for yourself. Luckily I did. I had to ask where Mel usually stood for corner kicks and Gary Speed told me to stand on the penalty spot. Before the corner he called out to me that I would score, and when the ball came over it seemed to be in the air for ages before I headed it in.'

	P	W	D	L	F	A	Pts
Leeds United	32	17	13	2	58	25	64
Manchester United	30	17	11	2	51	22	62
Sheffield Wed	31	15	9	7	50	42	54
Manchester City	32	15	8	9	45	39	53

Tottenham Hotspur: Thorstvedt, Fenwick, Van den Hauwe (Bergsson 46), Sedgley, Howells, Mabbutt, Stewart, Durie, Gray, Lineker (Walsh 17), Allen

Leeds United: Lukic, Sterland (Newsome 70), Whitlow (Cantona 76), Batty, Fairclough, Whyte, Strachan, Wallace, Chapman, McAllister, Speed

HEADS YOU LOSE! Jon Newsome heads Leeds back into the lead with a thumping header.

GO ON! Skipper Gordan Strachan urges Gary McAllister to win the ball in this duel.

CLEAN PUNCH! Erik Thorstvedt clears his lines as Leeds threaten his goal.

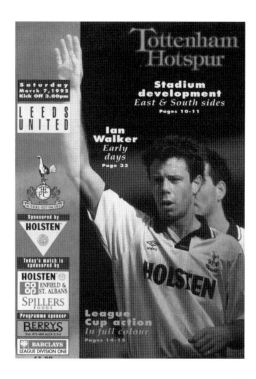

Queens Park Rangers v. Leeds United

11 March 1992   Football League, First Division
Loftus Road, London   Attendance: 14,641

This midweek fixture at Loftus Road gave Leeds an opportunity to build a five-point lead at the top of the table with Manchester United playing against Middlesborough in the Rumbelows Cup. Although Alex Ferguson's team would have three games in hand, such an advantage would put enormous pressure on them.

Howard Wilkinson was well aware that this would not be an easy game, as mid-table Rangers had all but ended Manchester City's slim title challenge following a resounding 4-0 win in their last outing. Nevertheless, the Leeds boss was convinced a healthy point's advantage would act as a psychological boost. With Mel Sterland and Mike Whitlow facing late tests, Wilkinson named a 16-man squad for their second trip to London in five days. Sterland failed, enabling Jon Newsome to make his first full appearance.

A STUNNING FOUR-GOAL DISPLAY by QPR sent Leeds crashing to their heaviest defeat of the season and possibly out of the title race.

The current league leaders are two points clear, but with Wembley-bound Manchester United having three games in hand, they are firmly in the 'box-seat' for the First Division championship. This result is a crushing blow for Howard Wilkinson's team, no matter how well meaning his brave words of defiance after the game.

During the early stages of this match there was no indication of the action that was to come as Leeds made the perfect start when Gary Speed powered home a great header from Jon Newsome's cross on 10 minutes. Indeed, the result could have been totally different had Lee Chapman not squandered a golden opportunity moments later.

The game turned when Wallace had to leave the field on 33 minutes for treatment to a head wound. Seizing on their numerical advantage Rangers equalised within four minutes after John Lukic had brilliantly turned an Andrew Impey shot round the post. From the

resultant corner taken by veteran Ray Wilkins, Les Ferdinand stabbed home from close range.

Wallace's return saw him blaze over before Gary McAllister wasted a great chance after being set up by Gordon Strachan on the stroke of half-time. The second half began with opportunities at both ends before Rangers took a firm grip on the match just after the hour when Wilkins set up Bradley Allen and Andy Sinton, both players finishing in some style.

Leeds' fate was sealed on 82 minutes when Chris Whyte was dismissed for a professional foul after conceding a penalty on Sinton; Clive Wilson sent Lukic the wrong way from the spot kick. There was no way back for Leeds, their title ambitions now hanging by a thread.

Referee: K. Cooper (Pontypridd)

Queens Park Rangers 4   Leeds United 1
Ferdinand, Allen,   *Speed*
Sinton, Wilson (Penalty)

WRONG-FOOTED! Clive Wilson ends a miserable evening for Leeds with a late penalty.

Howard Wilkinson, *Yorkshire Evening Post*: 'We've just got to keep on going. A lot of games remain. When people ask me about the championship I say I don't know what the outcome will be. I don't see anyone in the league surrendering in any game and I don't see anything to stop anyone stringing five or six wins together either. QPR played very well and deserved to win. They capitalised on our bad luck in the first half when Rod Wallace was off for a few minutes and in the second half they cashed in on our bad defensive display.'

	P	W	D	L	F	A	Pts
Leeds United	33	17	13	3	59	29	64
Manchester United	30	17	11	2	51	22	62
Sheffield Wed	32	15	9	8	51	45	54
Manchester City	32	15	8	9	45	39	53

Queens Park Rangers: Stejskal, Bardsley, Wilson, Impey, McDonald, Peacock, Wilkins, Holloway, Ferdinand, Allen, Sinton (Barker 86)
Leeds United: Lukic, Newsome, Whitlow, Batty, Fairclough, Whyte, Strachan, Wallace, Chapman, McAllister (Cantona 70), Speed

Leeds United v. Wimbledon

14 March 1992
Elland Road, Leeds

Football League, First Division
Attendance: 26,760

There was no time for Leeds players to brood over their heavy defeat to QPR. With a match against Wimbledon just 48 hours away, the team had a perfect opportunity to get back to winning ways. Eric Cantona was handed a place in the first team as Howard Wilkinson asked Gary Speed to again deputise at left-back in the continued absence of Tony Dorigo.

Howard Wilkinson, *Yorkshire Evening Post*: 'It's important that we bounce back and I believe we shall do. A lot of us at this club, including myself, have a lot of experience in football and we're not upset by setbacks. People like Lukic, Strachan, Sterland and Chapman have seen it all and done it all. They know what's needed. At times like these their experience and leadership will be a boon to their team-mates. It's a big prize they are playing for and they will give it everything.'

LEE CHAPMAN'S second treble of the campaign fired Leeds to a thrilling 5-1 win and proved the perfect tonic after their midweek setback. Leeds are still only two points clear after Manchester United's 2-1 victory at Sheffield United, but this result will set them in good heart for the battles that lay ahead.

The match got off to a slow start, but sprung into life midway through the first half when Leeds scored three times in eight minutes. Chapman grabbed the first two, side-footing home David Batty's centre after 23 minutes before clinically heading in Rod Wallace's astute cross four minutes later. Wallace then turned goalscorer on the half hour when he neatly finished off intricate play by Gordon Strachan. Leeds deservedly received a standing ovation at the interval, but they got off to a slow start in the second period without their inspirational skipper, Carl Shutt, having replaced him.

Wimbledon grabbed a goal on 51 minutes when ex-Leeds star Terry Phelan sent Paul Miller through on goal, Miller scoring at the second attempt after John Lukic had blocked his first effort, and almost scored a second when John Scales blazed over when clean through.

Teamwork however, has always been a feature of this Leeds team and they battled through a difficult patch before Eric Cantona made the game safe on 75 minutes with a brilliant finish after robbing Scales 60 yards from goal. Ten minutes from time, Chapman completed his hat-trick with a trademark header from Shutt's pinpoint cross to seal a fine win. The final scoreline may have been a shade flattering, but there can be no denying United's determination to take the title race to the wire.

Referee: K. Morton (Bury St Edmunds)

Howard Wilkinson, *Yorkshire Evening Post*: 'We're on course for the 84 points I felt would be sufficient to win the championship. If we reach that total we can't complain if someone does better and pips us for the prize.'

Leeds United 5
*Chapman (3), Wallace,
Cantona*

Wimbledon 1
Miller

BULLET HEADER! Chapman heads home his second goal.

Gary McAllister, *Yorkshire Evening Post*: 'Chappy just instinctively knows exactly where he should be all the time to get on the end of chances. Down the years he has perfected a happy knack of knocking in the goals with remarkable consistency. He does it so brilliantly.'

	P	W	D	L	F	A	Pts
Leeds United	34	18	13	3	64	30	67
Manchester United	31	18	11	2	53	23	65
Sheffield Wed	33	16	9	8	53	45	57
Manchester City	33	15	8	10	45	40	53

Leeds United: Lukic, Newsome, Cantona, Batty, Fairclough, Whyte, Strachan (Shutt 46), Wallace, Chapman, McAllister, Speed

Wimbledon: Segers, Hayes, Phelan, Barton, Scales, Fitzgerald, Miller, Earle, Fashanu (Clarke 74), Sanchez, McGee

Leeds United v. Wimbledon

Above: FOUL REF! Wimbledon's Warren Barton stops Gordon Strachan in full flight.

Left: HIGH FIVES! Gary McAllister congratulates Rod Wallace on his strike against the Dons.

22 March 1992	Football League, First Division
Highbury, London	Attendance: 27,844

Leeds received an unexpected boost when Manchester United lost the first of their three games in hand during a midweek fixture at Nottingham Forest thanks to a second-half goal from Nigel Clough.

Alex Ferguson, *Yorkshire Evening Post*: 'It was a very disappointing night for us, but a good result for Leeds. It will certainly give them more hope, although we have always been geared to the fact that the title race will go all the way. There are a lot of hard games to come for both sides and it's just a question of us getting our act together again as quickly as possible. It was one of those nights and we could have no complaint.'

Howard Wilkinson was philosophical about the sudden turnaround when the paper interviewed him. 'It's no use worrying about other results. We must just keep plugging away and hope things work out right for us in the end.' Following fitness tests, Gary Speed deputised for Mel Sterland with Jon Newsome returning to substitute duties.

A LATE EQUALISER from Paul Merson dented Leeds' title ambitions just when they could have taken a decisive step forward in this season's race.

In ordinary circumstances a draw at Highbury would be viewed as a good result, but with Manchester United drawing at home to Wimbledon 24 hours earlier, a Leeds win would have placed tremendous pressure on Alex Ferguson's team.

In a fiercely contested opening, chances were at a premium as defences dominated. The first half saw only two efforts of note, Merson going close for the home side with a thunderous shot, whilst Eric Cantona forced David Seaman into a breathtaking save after shrugging off Tony Adams challenge.

Leeds had to battle hard to stay in the game. The midfield trio of Gordon Strachan, David Batty and Gary McAllister were as industrious as ever, but nobody played better than central defenders Chris Fairclough and Chris Whyte who kept danger-man Ian Wright subdued. A stalemate seemed the likely outcome until Lee Chapman coolly scored after fine work by Rod Wallace on 74 minutes. This was the prolific striker's 19th goal of another productive season.

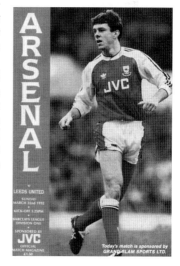

Gunners manager George Graham sent Ray Parlour and Anders Limpar on in a desperate bid to keep their flagging UEFA Cup hopes alive and it immediately paid off when Merson played a neat one-two with David O'Leary before twisting to equalise with a looped shot nine minutes from time. The goal was tough on Leeds who had battled hard and appeared to have done enough for what would have been a superb result, before one lack of concentration proved decisive.

Referee: M. Bodenham (Cornwall)

Arsenal 1	Leeds United 1
Merson	*Chapman*

DOUBLE ACT! Rod Wallace grabs Leeds' opening goal on the way to a much-needed win.

Howard Wilkinson, *Yorkshire Evening Post*: 'I still believe the championship will not be decided until almost the end of the season and obviously we're in with a good chance. I cannot fault my players. Remember, we started the season as fourth favourites and now we're top of the table. I set them a target of two points a game and we're only a fraction off that.'

	P	W	D	L	F	A	Pts
Leeds United	35	18	14	3	65	31	68
Manchester United	33	18	12	3	53	24	66
Sheffield Wed	34	17	9	8	54	45	60
Liverpool	33	14	13	6	38	29	55

Arsenal: Seaman, Dixon, Winterburn, Hillier (Parlour 78), Bould, Adams, Rocastle (Limpar 78), Wright, O'Leary, Merson, Campbell

Leeds United: Lukic, Cantona, Dorigo, Batty, McClelland, Whyte, Strachan, Wallace, Chapman, McAllister, Speed

LEEDS UNITED v. WEST HAM UNITED

28 March 1992
Elland Road, Leeds

Football League, First Division
Attendance: 31,101

With seven games remaining, Howard Wilkinson set a target of 16 or 17 points and confirmed that Mel Sterland would miss the rest of the season due to a persistent ankle injury. Speaking in the *Yorkshire Evening Post*, the Leeds manager said, 'The players are not afraid to go out and play, and I think that's what we should do right now. We must go out and enjoy the games.'

Wilkinson was forced to reshuffle his side against West Ham with Chris Whyte serving a one-match ban after his dismissal at QPR, but his side were firm favourites to comfortably defeat the relegation-threatened team who had collected just two points from their last eight games.

FOR THE SECOND TIME in three home matches Leeds drew a blank as another two points slipped away in their title quest. With Manchester United drawing at QPR, the league table remains unchanged, but this was a match Leeds should have won comfortably despite not being at their most fluent.

Throughout the opening period the players, as a unit, struggled to make inroads against a West Ham team rooted to the foot of the table; nevertheless there was no excuse for Lee Chapman's glaring miss on 20 minutes. Eric Cantona began the move setting David Batty clear down the right flank, but when his inch-perfect cross fell to United's leading marksman six-yards out, Chapman somehow mis-cued his shot past the post.

In Whyte's absence, Jon Newsome looked assured alongside Chris Fairclough, however, with Tony Dorigo at right-back and Gary Speed on the left, Leeds appeared unbalanced. After the break, Dorigo and Speed switched flanks. As a result Leeds looked more dangerous when they supported the attack, but the league leaders had not accounted for Hammers 'keeper Ludek Miklosko. The Czech international goalkeeper was in inspired form as he brilliantly saved Cantona's clever lob after a powerful run, before frustrating Newsome, Chapman and substitute Steve Hodge. Finally, Miklosko superbly tipped Gary McAllister's thumping 30-yard drive over the bar, leaving Leeds' supporters to ponder on the chances that had slipped away.

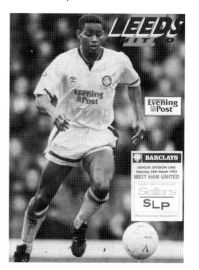

Referee: K. Barratt (Coventry)

Howard Wilkinson, *Yorkshire Evening Post*: 'I don't feel we are running out of games and things have not changed dramatically. We have had two very difficult games, and we came up against a very good goalkeeper against West Ham. My players are doing everything that could be asked of them. They have done it all season and I could not see how they could have done any more to try and win against West Ham. They defended well when it mattered.'

Leeds United 0   West Ham United 0

Leeds United v. West Ham United

WINGING IT! Rod Wallace tries to find a way past two West Ham defenders.

Alex Ferguson, following his side's draw at QPR, hinted in the *Yorkshire Evening Post* that Leeds were beginning to feel the pressure. 'They are showing nerves. It's only natural. A lot of their players haven't been there before but they're running out of games now.'

	P	W	D	L	F	A	Pts
Leeds United	36	18	15	3	65	31	69
Manchester United	34	18	13	3	53	24	67
Sheffield Wed	35	17	9	9	54	48	60
Liverpool	34	14	13	7	38	31	55

Leeds United: Lukic, Cantona, Dorigo, Batty, Fairclough, Newsome, Strachan, Wallace (Hodge 71), Chapman, McAllister, Speed

West Ham United: Miklosko, Brown, Dicks, Breacker, Foster, Potts, Bishop, Thomas, Small, Allen (Gate 36), Slater (McAvennie 83)

MANCHESTER CITY v. LEEDS UNITED

4 April 1992
Maine Road, Manchester

Football League, First Division
Attendance: 30,239

Manchester United put themselves back in pole position when they defeated Norwich City 3-1 in a midweek clash, taking them a point ahead of Leeds with a game in hand. Alex Ferguson, *Yorkshire Evening Post*: 'We are top with seven games to go. If we win these seven games we will be Champions, it is as simple as that. We have a hectic run-in with four games in six days but we have the players to handle it.'

Commenting on the result and his side's forthcoming clash at Maine Road, Howard Wilkinson told the *Yorkshire Evening Post*: 'As far as we are concerned we keep going. It is a long season and we still have 18 points to play for. A lot of water has still to flow under the bridge. We have operated all season in a certain way, playing relaxed, stylish, attacking football, and if we are going to end the season in the manner in which we deserve, we have got to keep on playing like that.'

A MIRACLE is now needed for Leeds United after this crushing defeat, and how ironic it will be if Manchester United's neighbours have inflicted the result, which settles the Championship.

With Alex Ferguson's team without a fixture, Leeds had a chance to once again put some pressure on the league leaders, but this was a day when their band of travelling supporters had little to cheer. Credit to City though, after a goalless four-match run they were determined to revive their own UEFA Cup ambitions and outshone Leeds in every department.

The match kicked off at 2 p.m. to mark the end of Ramadan and City were quick off the mark when Andy Hill powered home a header from Mark Brennan's corner after 11 minutes. The goal rocked Leeds. Stung into action, only Tony Coton's brilliant save from Gary Speed's flashing header and Brennan's desperate clearance off his goal line prevented an equaliser.

The home team though, playing with guile and spirit doubled their advantage when Mike Sheron neatly converted Steve McMahon's defence-splitting pass on 34 minutes.

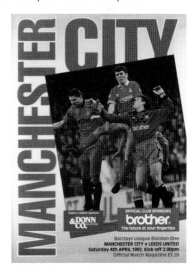

After the interval Leeds came out with all guns blazing, but after Wallace spooned a glorious chance over the bar, Coton again denied Leeds with a stunning save from Chris Fairclough's rising drive. An early goal would have given the visitors hope, but Niall Quinn finished the match as a contest on 62 minutes when he caught out John Lukic with a strike that went in off the underside of the crossbar. Five minutes from time Brennan sealed a fine victory for the Blues with a low-angled drive.

Bookmakers immediately slashed Manchester United's odds of winning a first title in 25 years to 8:1 on, with Leeds 9:2 against. Of more immediate concern to Leeds though is how the players will react to this defeat. They must also be getting concerned at how quickly Sheffield Wednesday, now six points adrift with a game in hand, have begun to catch them.

Manchester City 4
Hill, Sheron,
Quinn, Brennan

Leeds United 0

HEAD FIRST! David Batty looks like losing his head as well as the First Division title.

The Leeds boss will have his work cut out over the coming days, when he will have more than a passing interest in the result of the midweek Manchester derby.

Referee: J. Watson (Whitley Bay)

Howard Wilkinson, *Yorkshire Evening Post*: 'It is easy to go and applaud and take the bows when you have won and played well. We had 5,000 people at Maine Road and they have played their part this season. It was important that we acknowledged their support because when we were 4-0 down their support was very, very generous. Where it mattered, City did better than we did. In our penalty area we defended badly.'

Gordon Strachan, *Yorkshire Post:* 'We had our chance to stage a comeback but to dwell on our performance would be totally unfair to the way City played. If City play like that they are capable of winning anywhere, even at Old Trafford on Tuesday.'

Manchester City: Coton, Hill, Pointon, Brennan, Curle, Vonk, White, Sheron, Quinn (Brightwell 85), Simpson, McMahon
Leeds United: Lukic, Cantona, Dorigo, Batty, Fairclough, Whyte, Strachan, Wallace, Chapman, McAllister, Speed

Leeds United v. Chelsea

11 April 1992
Elland Road, Leeds

Football League, First Division
Attendance: 31,363

As the squad returned to training, David Batty summed up the players' mood in the *Yorkshire Evening Post:* 'We have not given up all hope, but you have to be realistic. As far as the championship is concerned it is now up to Manchester United. For our part we will strive to win all five of our remaining matches and to be honest I do not think that is beyond us. We are all looking forward to qualifying for Europe and if we can clinch a place in the UEFA Cup by finishing second in the league then it will have been a successful season for us.'

Just when Leeds' title ambitions appeared bleak, the club had a boost when the Manchester derby ended in a draw. Leeds' European ambitions were also improved when Sheffield Wednesday drew at Coventry City, leaving them five points adrift having played 37 games.

On the eve of the clash with Chelsea, Howard Wilkinson told the *Yorkshire Evening Post,* 'We have come a long way together and we are not about to let all the hard work go down the drain now. We have five games left in which we could boost our chances, and I would say we have to move back towards the identity we had at the start of the season. Now I feel it is important once more to nail our colours to the mast and go for it, re-establishing our old habits. The midweek results from Sheffield Wednesday and Manchester United have confirmed the championship is going to run its course to the final tape.'

The Leeds boss caused something of a surprise when he named Gary McAllister at right-back, allowing Gary Speed to return to midfield. With Steve Hodge back in the side and Eric Cantona on the bench, the team looked far more balanced than in recent weeks.

SUBSTITUTE ERIC CANTONA scored a magical goal on 89 minutes to seal a hard-fought win as Leeds once again went back to the top of the First Division.

This was a must-win game for Howard Wilkinson's team if they are to have any chance of winning the championship, especially with Manchester United not playing due to their participation in the Rumbelows Cup final. They now stand one point clear, having played two games more, but are back in the race although they need their Pennine rivals to slip up.

The first half was a bad-tempered affair, with no clear-cut chances for either side. Leeds felt aggrieved though after 17 minutes when referee Neil Midgley turned down their penalty appeals after Rod Wallace, having played a neat one-two with skipper Gordon Strachan, appeared to be bundled over by Steve Clarke.

David Batty was at his imposing best and Strachan was at the heart of everything, but with Paul Elliot commanding in defence there was no way through for the home side. The complexion of the game changed on 55 minutes when Leeds finally took the lead. Batty was involved in the build-up along with Lee Chapman, but it was Leeds' inspirational captain who made the goal with a strong run into the penalty area before finding Wallace, who beat Dave Beasant at the near post for his 11th goal of the campaign.

Suddenly, Leeds looked more assured but Chelsea battled away and made life difficult for their opponents. Wallace was proving a handful for Clarke in particular, who again appeared very fortunate not to concede a penalty after bringing down the nippy striker 20 minutes from time.

With five minutes to go Cantona replaced Hodge and within two minutes had helped

---

Leeds United 3
Wallace, Chapman
Cantona

Chelsea 0

LEEDS UNITED v. CHELSEA

VINNIE'S BACK! Vinnie Jones gets the better of Steve Hodge in a midfield tussle.

Leeds finally break the Londoners' resistance when Chapman grabbed his 20th goal of the season. Linking with Batty and Gary McAllister, Cantona set up Chapman who scored with his knee after his first shot had struck a post. His strike made him the first player since Peter Lorimer during the early 1970s to reach the 20-goal mark in successive seasons.

A minute from time the Frenchman conjured up the 'goal of the season' at Elland Road, in turn sending supporters home ecstatic. Receiving a quick throw-in from Strachan, the Frenchman flicked the ball over Elliot, controlled it in mid-air, beat the startled defender again before crashing home an unstoppable volley for a stunning goal. It was a piece of individual brilliance from a player of undoubted genius.

Although Leeds struggled for the best part of an hour, they have claimed three valuable points. Now they have to hope their great rivals drop points.

Referee: N. Midgley (Bolton)

Howard Wilkinson, *Yorkshire Post*: 'Today was more like what we are, playing in their half trying to win the ball back early. Not sophisticated tactically, just making them play in their half. That suits us at the moment in the stage of development we are at.'

Leeds United: Lukic, Hodge (Newsome 77), Dorigo, Batty, Fairclough, Whyte, Strachan, Wallace (Cantona 86), Chapman, McAllister, Speed

Chelsea: Beasant, Clarke (Dixon 71), Myers, Jones, Elliot, Monkou, Le Saux (Barnard 46), Townsend, Stuart, Cascarino, Wise

WALLOP! Rod Wallace grabs Leeds' opening goal on the way to a much-needed win.

	P	W	D	L	F	A	Pts
Leeds United	38	19	15	4	68	35	72
Manchester United	36	19	14	3	57	26	71
Sheffield Wed	38	19	10	9	58	48	67
Arsenal	38	17	13	8	70	43	64

NICE-LEE! Lee Chapman celebrates after scoring Leeds' second.

LIVERPOOL v. LEEDS UNITED

18 April 1992
Anfield, Liverpool

Football League, First Division
Attendance: 37,186

With key Easter fixtures coming up, Leeds faced Liverpool and Coventry City, but Manchester United's reserves of strength would be tested to the limit with four games in six days scheduled against Southampton, Luton Town, Nottingham Forest and West Ham. They claimed maximum points in the first with a hard-fought 1-0 win, a result taking them two points clear with a game in hand, but skipper Gordon Strachan was still hopeful that the title race would go to the end of the campaign.

Once again the Leeds manager decided to switch his team around in a bid to get the desired result. With Strachan rested, to preserve his energies for the battles ahead, Chris Fairclough played at right-back to mark Liverpool danger-man John Barnes. Jon Newsome came in at centre-back, enabling Gary McAllister to return to midfield.

LEEDS' TITLE AMBITIONS are still intact following an outstanding goalkeeping display by John Lukic, which could prove crucial in the final analysis.

Had Leeds recorded their first victory at Anfield in two decades, it would have been tough on the Anfield club as a draw was just about the right result. With Manchester United drawing at Luton Town, a two-point gap still remains between the two sides, leaving the destiny of the championship still in the balance.

Liverpool had little to play for, but true to their traditions did not make life easy for Leeds. Howard Wilkinson's reshaped team was effective in nullifying Barnes, but they did miss their inspirational skipper's presence in the side. Liverpool were dominant, especially in the first half, and the Leeds 'keeper was in action after 11 minutes when he made a flying save to deny Rush. Five minutes later he denied the Welsh international with a double-save, before stopping Ray Houghton in his tracks. In the second half although Leeds came into the game more, Mike Marsh, Barry Venison and Barnes were all frustrated by superb stops.

Leeds had their moments, but they were rare. Steve Hodge went close in the first half with a snap-shot, and late on they were agonisingly close to snatching a win when Rod Wallace forced Houghton to clear off his line, before substitute Eric Cantona saw his thumping shot just clear the bar.

This hard-earned point was gained by a sterling defensive effort. Everyone played a part as the Anfield team was kept at bay, but Man of the Match by some distance was Lukic who was simply sensational. In the end though, Leeds were satisfied to have gained a point; however with only three games remaining, time and matches are fast running out.

Referee: K. Redfern (Whitley Bay)

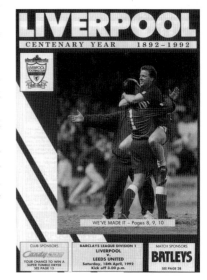

Liverpool 0   Leeds United 0

AGONY! Ray Houghton scrambles Chris Fairclough's shot off the line.

Howard Wilkinson, *Yorkshire Evening Post*: 'Obviously I would like to have won this game, but at this stage you cannot make unrealistic demands or go for unrealistic targets when you don't have to. I happen to think the situation is such that we don't have to, but if and when we have to go for all or nothing then we will go for it.'

Liverpool striker Dean Saunders *Yorkshire Evening Post*: 'Lukic was absolutely brilliant. I have never seen him play so well.'

	P	W	D	L	F	A	Pts
Manchester United	38	20	15	3	59	27	75
Leeds United	39	19	16	4	68	35	73
Sheffield Wed	38	20	10	9	59	48	70
Arsenal	39	17	14	8	71	44	65

Liverpool: Grobbelaar, Jones, Burrows, Nicol, Molby, Venison, Saunders, Houghton, Rush, Barnes, Thomas (Marsh 46)

Leeds United: Lukic, Newsome, Dorigo, Batty, Fairclough, Whyte, Hodge (Cantona 46), Wallace, Chapman, McAllister, Speed

LEEDS UNITED v. COVENTRY CITY

20 April 1992
Elland Road, Leeds

Football League, First Division
Attendance: 26,582

As expected there were no selection dilemmas for Howard Wilkinson with skipper Gordon Strachan back in the side, although Steve Hodge was ruled out after failing to shake off a knock picked up at Anfield.

Due to the match being broadcast live on ITV's *The Match*, supporters arrived for the 5 p.m. kick-off desperate for news of Manchester United's clash at home to Nottingham Forest. Following the final whistle after Forest's 2-1 win, Elland Road exploded. A victory against Coventry would take Leeds top by a point. A win was critical.

SECOND-HALF GOALS from Chris Fairclough and Gary McAllister edged Leeds ahead for the seventh time in one of the most extraordinary First Division championship races of all time. The 2-0 triumph was not straightforward as Coventry City, desperate for points to avoid relegation, battled throughout. The victory confirmed Leeds' return to European competition, but whether their destiny was the UEFA Cup or European Cup was still to be decided.

With so much at stake for both teams it was not surprising that the opening half was a cagey affair, with only two chances of note. Rod Wallace tested Coventry 'keeper Steve Ogrizovic after 11 minutes, and Jon Newsome stopped Kevin Gallacher in his tracks when clean through. Gallacher proved dangerous again early in the second half, but Chris Whyte blocked his first attempt, before John Lukic saved comfortably from the Scottish international.

The home team was playing controlled football and finally took the lead after 53 minutes when Whyte knocked Gordon Strachan's free kick across goal. Bryan Burrows, under intense pressure, mis-cued his clearance straight to Fairclough to head home. The goal brought a collective sigh of relief around the ground.

As the game opened up Gary Speed, Lee Chapman, McAllister and Wallace all went close before Leeds settled the match in controversial fashion when Lloyd McGrath was penalised for handling Eric Cantona's shot on the goal line with nine minutes remaining. The referee Bob Nixon was unsighted, but after consulting his linesman, who flagged the infringement, awarded a spot kick and dismissed McGrath for 'intentional hand-ball'. Coventry complained bitterly, but the decision stood. Television replays proved inconclusive. McAllister stepped up to calmly send Ogrizovic the wrong way. The goal signalled wild scenes of celebration as the battle for the title took another twist.

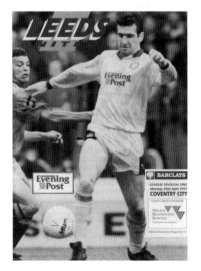

Referee: B. Nixon (West Kirby)

Howard Wilkinson, *Yorkshire Post*: 'We believe we can win the title but we know it depends on Manchester's results. We've got into Europe and that's terrific, but I wouldn't be thinking that we have a psychological edge if I was them.'

Leeds United 2
Fairclough
McAllister

Coventry City 0

HEADING FOR GLORY! Chris Fairclough soars to head Leeds into the lead.

THAT'LL DO! Gary McAllister salutes the Kop after his penalty clinched a vital win.

	P	W	D	L	F	A	Pts
Leeds United	40	20	16	4	70	35	76
Manchester United	39	20	15	4	60	29	75
Sheffield Wed	40	21	10	9	61	48	73
Arsenal	40	18	14	8	75	44	68

Leeds United: Lukic, Newsome, Dorigo, Batty, Fairclough, Whyte, Strachan (Shutt 83), Wallace (Cantona 75), Chapman, McAllister, Speed

Coventry City: Ogrizovic, Borrows, Sansom, Robson, Pearce, Atherton, Flynn, Gynn, Furlong (Ndlova 73), Gallacher (Emmerson 83), McGrath

SHEFFIELD UNITED v. LEEDS UNITED

26 April 1992   Football League, First Division
Bramall Lane, Sheffield   Attendance: 32,000

Two days after defeating Coventry City, Leeds United amazingly had the destiny of the championship in their hands after bottom-of-the-table West Ham sensationally toppled Manchester United (in the last of their games in hand) 1-0. A distraught Alex Ferguson told the *Yorkshire Evening Post;* 'Leeds are in the driving seat. It is as simple as that. It is the first time I've had to say that we now depend on others'. In 72 hours the title race had turned on it's head. Leeds were now 3-1 favourites, Manchester United, 9 to 4 on before the West Ham match, had moved out to 5 to 2 against. Leeds' permutations were straightforward. Victories over Sheffield United and Norwich City, or a win at Bramall Lane coupled with Liverpool defeating Ferguson's team at Anfield, would clinch the title.

Announcing a fully fit squad, Howard Wilkinson told the *Yorkshire Evening Post*, 'Obviously it's reassuring to know that it's now up to us. But no matter what the state of the First Division table is, the attitude of my players at Bramall Lane on Sunday will be no different from what it would have been had the game not been so crucial. They've worked hard all season to get where they are. They've done their best. They know I'm proud of them no matter what happens. My message to them is, keep playing and leave the comments and analysing to other people. You have to rely on your form, keep going and make sure you don't waste all the hard work already put in.'

IN ONE OF THE MOST EXTRAORDINARY GAMES in Leeds United's history, Brian Gayle's bizarre own goal not only clinched a 3-2 victory for Howard Wilkinson's team, but also handed them the First Division Championship.

PINBALL WIZARD! Rod Wallace nudges the ball past Mel Rees and Paul Beesley before Brian Gayle's clearance ricocheted off Speed and Wallace for Leeds' first goal.

Sheffield United 2   **Leeds United 3**
  Cork   *Wallace, Newsome*
  Chapman (Own Goal)   *Gayle (Own Goal)*

All three of Leeds' goals in an astonishing game had an element of good fortune about them, but the Championship is gained over a season, not in one game. For their dogged determination and perseverance in pursuit of the ultimate domestic honour, there can be no denying that Leeds United deserved this triumph, which was sealed a few hours later when Liverpool defeated Manchester United 2-0.

Ironically, but not particularly surprising in relation to the events of the day, Liverpool's victory meant that all three of the club's Division One titles (1968/69, 1973/74 and 1991/92) had been settled at Anfield.

The match kicked off at high noon in blustery conditions, which were interspersed with sporadic April showers. Leeds fielded an unchanged line-up for the first time since February, but the early stages saw the home side look far more comfortable. Both Brian Deane and Alan Cork troubled Leeds' central defenders and John Pemberton found plenty of space in midfield.

Pemberton nearly opened the scoring on 10 minutes with a fine shot that Chris Whtye only just cleared off the line, but with mounting pressure Dave Basset's team deservedly opened the scoring on 29 minutes following their seventh corner by John Gannon. Chris Fairclough cleared the initial danger, but when Glyn Hodges played the ball back across the penalty box, Cork prodded the ball home after it deflected to him off Gordon Strachan's boot.

TURNING POINT! Gary Speed and Gary McAllister congratulate Rod Wallace on his bizarre equalizer.

Leeds struggled to make inroads, although David Batty was at his combative best and Gary Speed looked sharp, but Lee Chapman and Rod Wallace were both subdued in attack. Just when it seemed Sheffield United would have an interval lead Leeds bounced back deep into injury time following a quickly taken free-kick by Strachan some 40 yards from goal. Spotting Wallace free, Strachan's instinctive pass caught Sheffield's defence flat. Wallace raced through to get the faintest of touches as Blades 'keeper Mel Rees and Paul Beesley collided. Brian Gayle was first to react, but his attempted clearance saw the ball 'pinball style' hit Speed and strike Wallace on the thigh before flying off at a right-angle into the net past Pemberton stranded on the goal line.

Rees needed lengthy treatment and the goal was the last action of an exciting half. The Sheffield 'keeper bravely re-emerged with his leg heavily strapped and mobility severely restricted. Strachan though was less fortunate as Steve Hodge replaced him at the start of the second half. The skipper's ingenuity however had changed the course of the match.

With the wind at their backs there was a marked improvement in Leeds performance and just after the hour the game shifted their way, moments after John Lukic had made a brilliant double-save from Deane. Gaining possession, Leeds attacked with pace until Pemberton

Sheffield United: Rees, Pemberton, Barnes, Gannon (Whitehouse 76), Gayle, Beesley, Hodges, Rogers, Cork (Bryson 80), Deane, Bradshaw

Leeds United: Lukic, Newsome, Dorigo, Batty, Fairclough, Whyte, Strachan (Shutt 46), Wallace, Chapman, McAllister (Cantona 76), Speed

fouled Batty on the edge of the penalty box. Weighing up his options, Gary McAllister superbly floated a cross beyond everyone to Jon Newsome at the far post, who stooped to nod in unchallenged. Rees had tried to get to the ball but got nowhere near due to his injury.

Leeds' joy though was short-lived. On 67 minutes, following another Gannon corner, Pemberton fired the ball across the face of the goal. In his efforts to clear the danger, Chapman inadvertently diverted the ball into his own net to send this intriguing match into the melting pot once again.

Pemberton soon had Leeds back-peddling again with a fine run and shot that only just cleared the bar, prompting Wilkinson to bring Eric Cantona on for McAllister with 12 minutes to go. The substitution paid dividends within sixty seconds as the Frenchman helped Leeds take the lead for a second time. Chasing his own long clearance downfield with Wallace, Gayle under intense pressure from the pair tried to head clear, but underestimating the distance his crocked 'keeper had travelled, looped the ball over him and into the unguarded net.

Leeds had the lead and they were not going to lose their slender advantage again. Defending with authority they held on without too many scares to record a priceless win. By late afternoon the title race was officially over following Liverpool's victory. On a day of raw nerves and ceaseless excitement, Wilkinson's team had come through the most searching of tests and a city began its celebrations.

Referee: G. Courtney (Spennymoor)

Howard Wilkinson gave numerous interviews following the victory at Bramall Lane. They included:

Daily Express: 'To say it was an uneventful match is an absolute understatement. There were more than a few heart-stopping moments. I don't think we could have chosen a more difficult place to come and win. Career-wise this is the most fantastic day of my life, one of those days when dreams come true.'

Daily Mail: 'Given the wind, Sheffield United's form, ability in the air and deadliness at set pieces, it was always going to be like that. A lot of sides have caved in there recently. The players have been magnificent. I never felt we would fall away, even if I did believe it would go right to the final day of the season.'

The Sun: 'We came here to win and only win. This Sheffield United side was the First Division's form team. We knew it would be difficult but there was no question that we went out for three points and we got them. A lot of people would have come here for a draw. That is satisfying for my players and me. It was pleasing the final period produced the best football of the afternoon and that was when we got a grip of it. Before the game I thought if we would get a draw here, it would be a good result, so you can imagine how I felt at the end.'

Gordon Strachan, *Yorkshire Evening Post* Captain's Column (27 April 1992): 'Winning the League Championship is a tremendous achievement for Leeds United and especially so when you stop to consider that only four years ago the club was in the depths of the Second Division. It is a tribute to the management skills of Howard Wilkinson and, of course, the ability and dedication of the players who have battled through the long hard months of a First Division campaign and come out on top. I feel privileged to have been captain of the side that has brought this major trophy back to Elland Road.'

Alex Ferguson, *Daily Mail*: 'It's terribly disappointing to end this way, but there's no point analysing ourselves now. I think we have to say well done to Howard Wilkinson. It's marvellous for him, people say it's an ordinary league but that's absolute nonsense. It's the same hard league it's always been. Leeds deserve their achievement because they have worked hard. We at United congratulate them on that.'

MY BALL! Jon Newsome makes the score 2-1.

	P	W	D	L	F	A	Pts
Leeds United	41	21	16	4	73	37	79
Manchester United	41	20	15	6	60	32	75
Sheffield Wed	41	21	11	9	62	49	74
Arsenal	41	18	15	8	76	45	69

YES! Jon Newsome celebrates his goal with Chris Fairclough and Gary Speed.

OOPS! Brian Gayle's header is on its way into the net for Leeds' winner.

EYES RIGHT! Mel Rees, Brian Gayle, Eric Cantona and Rod Wallace watch the ball sail into an empty net for Leeds' winning goal and ultimately the First Division Championsip.

LUCKY LEEDS! Wallace and Cantona cannot believe their good fortune as Leeds take a 3-2 lead.

LEEDS UNITED v. NORWICH CITY

2 May 1992
Elland Road, Leeds

Football League, First Division
Attendance: 32,673

As players relaxed, David Batty was named Leeds United's 'Player of the Year', whilst Tony Dorigo picked up the Supporters' Club 'Player of the Year' award.

During the week Howard Wilkinson told the *Yorkshire Evening Post*: 'We cannot pretend that the Norwich game has no significance because as far as I am concerned it has. We are unbeaten at home in the league and I want to see it stay that way. At the start of the season I set us a target to average two points per game, I would like to see us finish with as near to that as possible. I knew when I set that target it would be very difficult to achieve and that it would mean the players straining every nerve and sinew, and playing to the very limit of their ability. If we can beat Norwich we will finish the campaign only two points short of the target I set, and that in itself would be a tremendous achievement. With these things in mind it is important that we get down to some training in readiness for the game. There are many things about tomorrow that are absolutely different to anything we have come up against this season, but when kick off comes we have to think about a football match and the players owe it to themselves to make sure the whole of tomorrow afternoon is top quality.'

With demand for tickets far exceeding supply, a capacity attendance of 33,500 would witness Gordon Strachan become the last captain of a top-flight club to receive the 104-year-old League Championship trophy.

A SENSATIONAL SOLO GOAL by Rod Wallace rounded off Leeds' title-winning campaign in style before a capacity crowd at Elland Road. The match overall may not have been a classic but the carnival atmosphere throughout was unforgettable and in line with Wallace's strike.

The win meant Leeds finished four points clear of their nearest rivals Manchester United and preserved their unbeaten home record in the league, the only team to accomplish the feat. Their four defeats was also the lowest of any side during the campaign.

With thousands of supporters locked outside the ground, the afternoon proceedings began 45 minutes before kick-off with entertainment from marching bands. As the atmosphere built, the team finally entered onto the pitch to a crescendo of noise, fireworks and an impromptu ticker tape welcome for the trophy presentation.

After chairman Leslie Silver was presented with a Barclays League cheque for £100,000, skipper Gordon Strachan received the famous championship trophy from Football League president Gordon McKeag. Raising it to rapturous applause, the trophy was passed down the line of players to continued cheers. Addressing the crowd manager Howard Wilkinson said, 'The players have been absolutely magnificent. The League Championship is one of the most difficult tasks in football, certainly in Europe, if not the world.'

With Strachan on the bench, Eric Cantona started the game and David Batty wore the captain's armband. Leeds controlled the early phases of the game with Jon Newsome, Cantona and Lee Chapman all forcing saves from 'keeper Mark Walton, before Wallace's moment of magic on 25 minutes. There was nothing on when Wallace picked up Speed's pass in the centre circle, but the club's record signing proceeded to ghost past Jeremy Goss, thread his way past three further defenders before gliding his left-foot shot past a helpless Walton. It was a moment of pure genius that the occasion deserved.

Leeds United 1
Wallace

Norwich City 0

Leeds United v. Norwich City

GLORY RUN! Rod Wallace weaves his way towards a sensational solo goal.

The visitors tried to respond. Robert Fleck and Ruel Fox troubled Leeds defence intermittently, and Fleck almost got his reward when he forced an acrobatic save from John Lukic, clearly determined to keep a 20th clean sheet. Goss went close again early in the second half, but Leeds almost grabbed a second from Cantona, only for the alert Walton to tip his blistering volley round the post on 52 minutes.

Fifteen minutes from time Chapman and Cantona left the field to a standing ovation, which continued, when Strachan and Steve Hodge replaced them. Batty immediately handed back the captain's armband to his skipper, who almost grabbed a second when the Norwich 'keeper held his stinging shot with some difficulty. Leeds played out the remaining minutes with comfort to complete their 22nd victory of the season.

Throughout the match the crowd had been in fine voice, mixing their celebrations with numerous 'Mexican waves'. As Norwich departed, the scene was set for the Leeds squad to enjoy one final lap of honour as the capacity crowd stayed behind to savour the atmosphere and end a perfect day.

Referee: R. Milford (Bristol)

Leeds United: Lukic, Newsome, Dorigo, Batty, Fairclough, Whyte, Cantona (Strachan 75), Wallace, Chapman (Hodge 75), McAllister, Speed

Norwich City: Walton, Culverhouse, Ullathorne (Woodthorpe 78), Blades, Polston, Goss, Fox, Fleck, Newman, Johnson, Phillips

EASY FINISH! Rod Wallace finishes off his season in style.

THAT'LL DO NICELY!

CHAMPIONS!

YOU BEAUTY! Steve Hodge takes his turn to lift the famous old trophy.

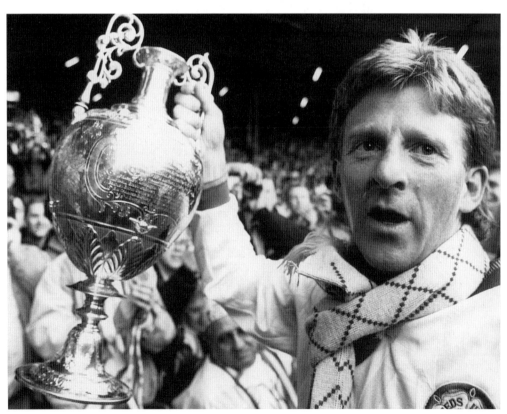

CAPTAIN SUPREME! Gordon Strachan shows off the trophy during the lap of honour.

IT'S OURS!

	P	W	D	L	F	A	Pts
Leeds United	42	22	16	4	74	37	82
Manchester United	42	21	15	6	63	33	78
Sheffield Wed	42	21	12	9	62	49	75
Arsenal	42	19	15	8	81	46	72
Manchester City	42	20	10	12	61	48	70
Liverpool	42	16	16	10	47	40	64
Aston Villa	42	17	9	16	48	44	60
Nottingham Forest	42	16	11	15	60	58	59
Sheffield United	42	16	9	17	65	63	57
Crystal Palace	42	14	15	13	53	61	57
QPR	42	12	18	12	48	47	54
Everton	42	13	14	15	52	51	53
Wimbledon	42	13	14	15	53	53	53
Chelsea	42	13	14	15	50	60	53
Tottenham	42	15	7	20	58	63	52
Southampton	42	14	10	18	39	55	52
Oldham Athletic	42	14	9	19	63	67	51
Norwich City	42	11	12	19	47	63	45
Coventry City	42	11	11	20	35	44	44
Luton Town	42	10	12	20	38	71	42
Notts County	42	10	10	22	40	62	40
West Ham United	42	9	11	22	37	59	38

Victory Parade and Civic Reception

Twenty-four hours after collecting the Championship trophy, over 150,000 people lined the streets of Leeds city centre during May Bank Holiday Sunday for the club's victory parade. Winding their way from Elland Road to the heart of the city, the players and manager congregated at the City Art Gallery in the Headrow where they saluted supporters. After addressing the crowd to tumultuous applause, the party attended a civic reception.

By the last game 618,269 spectators had attended the 21 home league fixtures, an average 29,441 and the highest since 1976/77. John Lukic was the only ever-present in all 49 league and cup matches. Chris Whyte missed one game, Gary McAllister and Gary Speed missed two. In all, 25 players represented the first team during the season. Lee Chapman once again topped the scoring charts with 20 goals. In all 15 players scored goals, and the team benefited from three own goals.

After winning manager of the month awards in October and November, less than a fortnight after clinching the Championship, Howard Wilkinson was named Barclays Football Manager of the Year. He was presented with a £5,000 cheque at a lunch organised by the Football League at London's Savoy Hotel.

THANKS FOR YOUR SUPPORT!

Class of '92

Howard Wilkinson, manager: Played for Sheffield Wednesday and Brighton before coaching Boston United. Guided Notts County and Sheffield Wednesday to promotion before leading Leeds United to the Second Division title in 1989/90. Organised, deep thinking and hardworking, 'Wilko' was 'Manager of the Year' after guiding Leeds to the First Division crown in 1991/92.

David Batty, midfield: Key member of 1989/90 promotion team. Leeds-born, Batty was renowned for his strong tackling, fierce determination and never-say-die attitude. Scored unforgettable goals during '92 campaign against Manchester City and Notts County. 42 England caps. Appearances: 40. Goals: 2.

Eric Cantona, forward: Joined Leeds in February 1992 to strengthen attacking options. Mainly used as a substitute, but Leeds fans witnessed his genius with a 'wonder' goal against Chelsea during title run-in. Appearances: 6 (9). Goals: 3.

Lee Chapman, centre-forward: Joined Leeds for £400,000 in January 1989, his goals helped clinch promotion to Division One in 1989/90. Superb in the air and brave, Chapman was a natural leader of the line. Top scorer in 1991/92, including hat-tricks against Sheffield Wednesday and Wimbledon. Appearances: 38. Goals: 16.

Tony Dorigo, left-back: Joined Leeds for £1.3m in July 1991. A brilliant timer of tackles, Dorigo possessed tremendous pace with an eye for a spectacular goal, as his majestic strikes against Manchester City and at Norwich City during debut season illustrated. 15 England caps. Appearances: 38. Goals: 3.

Chris Fairclough, centre-half: Joined Leeds for £500,000 in March 1989. Stalwart defender in 1989/90 promotion campaign. Tremendous pace, positional play and heading ability. Scored crucial goal against Coventry City during title run-in. Appearances: 30 (1). Goals: 2.

Steve Hodge, midfield: Joined Leeds for £900,000 in August 1991. Strong, skilful and possessed a striker's instinct in the penalty box. Influenced many games with cameo appearances. Debut goal against Sheffield Wednesday and memorable winner against Liverpool. 24 England caps. Appearances: 12 (11). Goals: 7.

John Lukic, goalkeeper: Made debut in 1979 before winning League title with Arsenal prior to £1m transfer to Leeds in June 1990. Commanding in the box, a terrific shot-stopper and brilliant reflexes. Lukic was the only ever present during '92 campaign. Outstanding throughout season, best demonstrated at Anfield. Appearances: 42.

Gary McAllister, midfield: Joined Leeds for £1m in June 1990. An elegant player with exceptional passing ability, McAllister was an expert at dead-ball situations and possessed a powerful shot. Scored a scorcher at Notts County and a vital penalty against Coventry City during title run-in. Captained Scotland, 58 caps. Appearances: 41 (1). Goals: 5.

John McClelland, centre-half: Joined Leeds for £100,000 in June 1989. Deputised at right-back and centre-half during early stages of '92 campaign, never letting the team down. Excellent in the air, used his experience to read dangerous situations. Captained Northern Ireland, 55 caps. Appearances: 16 (2).

Jon Newsome, right-back: Joined Leeds for combined fee of £275,000 in May 1991. Played mainly at left-back during last third of '92 campaign, bringing balance to the side. Scored a crucial goal at Sheffield United in match that decided title. Appearances: 7 (3). Goals: 2.

Carl Shutt, forward: Joined Leeds for £50,000 in March 1989. Member of 1989/90 promotion squad, Shutt was quick and a fine finisher. Deputised for Rod Wallace when injured during the early part of '92 season, scoring winner at Chelsea. Appearances: 6 (8). Goals 1.

Gary Speed, midfield: Broke into first team during 1989/90 promotion campaign. Brilliant in the air, especially at set pieces, Speed scored his quota of goals during '92 campaign, none better than a blockbuster at Southampton, in additon to demonstrating his versatility in a variety of positions. Captained Wales, 68 caps. Appearances: 41. Goals: 7.

Mel Sterland, right-back: Joined Leeds for £600,000 in July 1989. Key member of 1989/90 promotion team, 'Zico' was courageous, superb at timing tackles, an excellent crosser of the ball and had a fearsome shot. His six goals during '92 campaign included a crucial penalty against Manchester United. 1 England cap. Appearances: 29 (2). Goals: 6.

Gordon Strachan, midfield and captain: Joined Leeds for £300,000 in March 1989. Key player in renaissance of club. Top scorer in 1989/90 promotion campaign, 'Football of the Year' in 1990/91, his leadership, motivational and footballing skills made him indispensable. Scored four penalties in opening six games of '92 season. Captained Scotland, 50 caps. Appearances: 35 (1). Goals: 4.

Rod Wallace, forward: Striker. Joined Leeds for a club record £1.6m in June 1991. Lightning pace, skilful and elusive. Wallace was a handful for any defence. Clinical in front of goal as he demonstrated against Everton and at Norwich City. Scored vital goal at Sheffield United in match that decided title. Appearances: 34. Goals: 11.

Mike Whitlow, left-back: Joined Leeds for £30,000 in November 1988. Member of 1989/90 promotion squad, solid tackler and fine passer of the ball, Scored in 6-1 win at Sheffield Wednesday. Appearances: 3 (7). Goals: 1.

Chris Whyte, centre-half: Joined Leeds for £450,000 in June 1990. Determined stopper, affectionately nicknamed 'Huggy'. Fine header of the ball and excellent at making well-judged tackles and blocks. During '92 campaign scored at Notts County. Appearances: 41. Goals: 1.

Also played: Tony Agana 1(1), David Wetherall (1), Chris Kamara (2), Bobby Davison (2), Imre Varadi 2 (1) and Gary Kelly (2)

Statistics are for First Division; substitute appearances are in brackets.
International caps are career totals.

1991/92 – LEAGUE FIRST DIVISION

DATE	VENUE	OPPONENTS	SCORE	RESULT	GOALSCORERS	ATTENDANCE
20 Aug	HOME	NOTTINGHAM FOREST	1-0	W	McALLISTER	29,457
24 Aug	HOME	SHEFFIELD WEDNESDAY	1-1	D	HODGE	30,260
28 Aug	AWAY	SOUTHAMPTON	4-0	W	SPEED 2, STRACHAN 2 (2P)	15,847
31 Aug	AWAY	MANCHESTER UNITED	1-1	D	CHAPMAN	43,778
03 Sep	HOME	ARSENAL	2-2	D	STRACHAN (P), CHAPMAN	29,396
07 Sep	HOME	MANCHESTER CITY	3-0	W	DORIGO, BATTY, STRACHAN (P)	29,986
14 Sep	AWAY	CHELSEA	1-0	W	SHUTT	23,439
18 Sep	AWAY	COVENTRY CITY	0-0	D		15,488
21 Sep	HOME	LIVERPOOL	1-0	W	HODGE	32,917
28 Sep	AWAY	NORWICH CITY	2-2	D	DORIGO, SPEED	15,828
01 Oct	AWAY	CRYSTAL PALACE	0-1	L		18,298
05 Oct	HOME	SHEFFIELD UNITED	4-3	W	HODGE 2, STERLAND 2 (1P)	28,362
19 Oct	AWAY	NOTTS COUNTY	4-2	W	CHAPMAN, HODGE, WHYTE, McALLISTER	12,964
26 Oct	HOME	OLDHAM ATHLETIC	1-0	W	O.G. (KILCLINE)	28,199
02 Nov	AWAY	WIMBLEDON	0-0	D		7,025
16 Nov	HOME	QUEENS PARK RANGERS	2-0	W	STERLAND, WALLACE	27,087
24 Nov	AWAY	ASTON VILLA	4-1	W	WALLACE, STERLAND, CHAPMAN 2	23,666
30 Nov	HOME	EVERTON	1-0	W	WALLACE	30,043
07 Dec	AWAY	LUTON TOWN	2-0	W	WALLACE, SPEED	11,550
14 Dec	AWAY	TOTTENHAM HOTSPUR	1-1	D	SPEED	31,404
22 Dec	AWAY	NOTTINGHAM FOREST	0-0	D		27,170
26 Dec	HOME	SOUTHAMPTON	3-3	D	HODGE 2, SPEED	29,053
29 Dec	HOME	MANCHESTER UNITED	1-1	D	STERLAND (P)	32,638
01 Jan	AWAY	WEST HAM UNITED	3-1	W	CHAPMAN 2, McALLISTER	21,766
12 Jan	AWAY	SHEFFIELD WEDNESDAY	6-1	W	CHAPMAN 3, DORIGO, WHITLOW, WALLACE	32,228
18 Jan	HOME	CRYSTAL PALACE	1-1	D	FAIRCLOUGH	27,717
01 Feb	HOME	NOTTS COUNTY	3-0	W	STERLAND, BATTY, WALLACE	27,224
08 Feb	AWAY	OLDHAM ATHLETIC	0-2	L		18,409
23 Feb	AWAY	EVERTON	1-1	D	O.G. (KEOWN)	19,248
29 Feb	HOME	LUTON TOWN	2-0	W	CANTONA, CHAPMAN	28,231
03 Mar	HOME	ASTON VILLA	0-0	D		28,896
07 Mar	AWAY	TOTTENHAM HOTSPUR	3-1	W	WALLACE, NEWSOME, McALLISTER	27,622
11 Mar	AWAY	QUEENS PARK RANGERS	1-4	L	SPEED	14,641
14 Mar	AWAY	WIMBLEDON	5-1	W	CHAPMAN 3, WALLACE, CANTONA	26,760
22 Mar	AWAY	ARSENAL	1-1	D	CHAPMAN	27,844
28 Mar	HOME	WEST HAM UNITED	0-0	D		31,101
04 Apr	AWAY	MANCHESTER CITY	0-4	L		30,239
11 Apr	HOME	CHELSEA	3-0	W	WALLACE, CHAPMAN, CANTONA	31,363
18 Apr	AWAY	LIVERPOOL	0-0	D		37,186
20 Apr	HOME	COVENTRY CITY	2-0	W	FAIRCLOUGH, McALLISTER (P)	26,582
26 Apr	AWAY	SHEFFIELD UNITED	3-2	W	WALLACE, NEWSOME, O.G. (GAYLE)	32,000
02 May	HOME	NORWICH CITY	1-0	W	WALLACE	32,673

PLD	W	D	L	F	A	W	D	L	F	A	PTS	POS
42	13	8	0	38	13	9	8	4	36	24	82	1ST

1991/92 – CUP MATCHES

DATE	VENUE	OPPONENTS	SCORE	RESULT	GOALSCORERS	ATTENDANCE
15 Jan	HOME	MANCHESTER UNITED (R3)	0-1	L		31,819
LEAGUE CUP						
24 Sept	AWAY	SCUNTHORPE (R2)	0-0	D		8,392
08 Oct	HOME	SCUNTHORPE (R2)	3-0	W	STERLAND (P), CHAPMAN, SPEED	14,558
29 Oct	HOME	TRANMERE ROVERS (R3)	3-1	W	CHAPMAN 2, SHUTT	18,266
04 Dec	AWAY	EVERTON	4-1	W	SPEED, CHAPMAN, WALLACE 2	25,467
08 Jan	HOME	MANCHESTER UTD (R5)	1-3	L	SPEED	28,866

LEEDS UNITED ALSO PLAYED IN THE ZENITH DATA SYSTEMS CUP

LEAGUE

	APPS	SUBS	GOALS
LUKIC	42	0	0
McLELLAND	16	2	0
DORIGO	38	0	3
BATTY	40	0	2
FAIRCLOUGH	30	1	2
WHYTE	41	0	1
STRACHAN	35	1	4
R. WALLACE	34	0	11
CHAPMAN	38	0	16
McALLISTER	41	1	5
SPEED	41	0	7
HODGE	12	11	1
STERLAND	29	2	6
WETHERALL	0	1	0
SHUTT	6	8	1
VARADI	2	1	0
WHITLOW	3	7	1
KAMARA	0	2	0
NEWSOME	7	3	2
KELLY	0	2	0
DAVISON	0	2	0
CANTONA	6	9	3
AGANA	1	1	0
WILLIAMS	0	0	0

FA CUP

	APPS	SUBS	GOALS
LUKIC	1	0	0
McLELLAND	0	0	0
DORIGO	1	0	0
BATTY	1	0	0
FAIRCLOUGH	1	0	0
WHYTE	1	0	0
STRACHAN	0	1	0
R. WALLACE	1	0	0
CHAPMAN	1	0	0
McALLISTER	1	0	0
SPEED	1	0	0
HODGE	0	0	0
STERLAND	1	0	0
WETHERALL	0	0	0
SHUTT	0	0	0
VARADI	0	0	0
WHITLOW	0	0	0
KAMARA	0	1	0
NEWSOME	0	0	0
KELLY	0	0	0
DAVISON	0	1	0
CANTONA	0	0	0
AGANA	0	0	0
WILLIAMS	0	0	0

LEAGUE CUP

	APPS	SUBS	GOALS
LUKIC	5	0	0
McLELLAND	2	1	0
DORIGO	5	0	0
BATTY	4	0	0
FAIRCLOUGH	3	1	0
WHYTE	5	0	0
STRACHAN	4	0	0
R. WALLACE	3	0	2
CHAPMAN	5	0	4
McALLISTER	4	0	0
SPEED	4	0	3
HODGE	3	2	0
STERLAND	5	0	1
WETHERALL	0	0	0
SHUTT	2	1	1
VARADI	0	1	0
WHITLOW	0	1	0
KAMARA	0	0	0
NEWSOME	0	1	0
KELLY	0	0	0
DAVISON	0	1	0
CANTONA	0	0	0
AGANA	0	0	0
WILLIAMS	1	1	0